01/07

13º

Detours

BY RICHARD LA PLANTE
from Tom Doherty Associates

Detours

Life, Death, and Divorce
on the Road to Sturgis

RICHARD LA PLANTE

A TOM DOHERTY ASSOCIATES BOOK

NEW YORK

DETOURS: LIFE, DEATH, AND DIVORCE
ON THE ROAD TO STURGIS

Copyright © 2002 by Richard La Plante

This book is printed on acid-free paper.

Book design by Mark Abrams

A Forge Book
Published by Tom Doherty Associates, LLC
175 Fifth Avenue
New York, NY 10010

www.tor.com

Forge® is a registered trademark of Tom Doherty Associates, LLC.

Library of Congress Cataloging-in-Publication Data

La Plante, Richard.
    Detours: life, death, and divorce on the road to Sturgis/Richard La Plante.—1st ed.
      p.cm.
    "A Tom Doherty Associates book."
    ISBN 0-765-30324-8
    1. La Plante, Richard.   2. Motorcylclists—United States—Biography.
3. Motorcycling—United States.   4. Sturgis Rally and Races.   I. Title.

GV1060.2.L 32 A3 2002
796.7'5'092—dc21
[B]
                               2002069258

First Edition: September 2002

Printed in the United States of America

0 9 8 7 6 5 4 3 2 1

This book is for Betina, Jack, and Tomas

Thanks to:

Big Dog Motorcycles
Warrs' Harley-Davidson
Nat Sobel
Bob Gleason
Tom Doherty
Smitty Banditti
Jim Bush
Bill V.
Escargot
Stamp
Jean, Heather, Melissa, Shauna, Kaitlin
Christopher K.
Lee W.
and
Everyone who has made this book possible
by either being in it,
or riding a motorcycle.

Detours

BEGINNING, AGAIN

FORTY IS THE OLD AGE OF YOUTH,
FIFTY IS THE YOUTH OF OLD AGE.

—VICTOR HUGO

THE LAST TIME

August, 1997

I'M STANDING BY THE SIDE OF THE ROAD with my feet spread and my hands on top of my head. There's a cop on either side of me and a particularly zealous one shining the beam from a flashlight into my eyes, his muscular arms popping from the short sleeves of his shirt.

"You carrying any weapons," he asks brusquely. "A gun or a knife?"

"No, sir," I reply, having learned over the years that officers of the law like to be called "sir." Even though I'm twice this guy's age.

I'm not having a bad time, not yet, just a little uncomfortable in this position, watching hundreds of motorcycles cruise by, their riders rubbernecking to see who the unlucky stiff is, assuming the position.

Then the pat-down begins. Flashlight in face, I'm nearly blind as one of the other cops begins a full body rub, from my boots, up my calves and thighs, over the pockets on the back of my jeans, a little pat on my ass, and up and across my chest where his hand stops.

"What's that?" he asks.

"What's what?"

"You've got something in the pocket of your jacket," he announces. "What are you carrying?"

"I don't know," I answer, and at that moment, I actually don't. Its been a long, long day, beginning at seven o'clock with a broken ignition wire followed by a ride into Sturgis, a trip to the tattoo studio, a drink at Big Bertha's with a bikini-clad lady wearing an eight-foot python for a necklace, a few margaritas at a Mexican restaurant in Spearfish, followed by a book signing session at the Armory, followed by a ride to Deadwood. Now we've got to get home.

"Don't move," a voice says from somewhere beyond the glare.

The mood of the evening shifts from lukewarm to ice-cold as I hear the snap of holsters opening. Suddenly I'm having a very bad time. I know I don't have a gun on me but carrying anything that can be construed as (drug) paraphernalia can get you fined or locked up. Does a Bic lighter count?

My own bike is parked a few yards away from me, missing a taillight, which is the reason we were stopped in the first place. It's also sporting a rather unusual license plate. It is orange and black with the letters JGJ. It's a British plate but the bike's about as American as it gets, an '89 Harley Springer. I never thought I'd see this particular bike again. I left it in London in 1995, along with an eighteen-year marriage.

While I departed the country the Springer stayed at Warrs' Harley-Davidson, England's oldest bike dealers and

my good friends—in my mid-life biking career I must have
dropped enough money there to build them a new showroom, a shrine in polished wood and custom chrome. I
put a price tag on the bike of $35,000.00 and figured it
would be gone before I'd touched down in New York. A
few months later I got a call from John Warr. "Richard,
we've got a shipment of new bikes coming in and no room
for them on the floor. Besides, it's taking a full team to
keep yours polished. What do you want me to do with it?"

A biking friend, Jess, came to my rescue, volunteering
his garage. Warrs took care of the transport and the
Springer was banished to a lock-up in Surrey, near Brighton by the Sea.

I tried like hell to sell that Springer to Jess. It wasn't
that I didn't love it. I did. The damn thing was even mentioned in my divorce case, as the other woman, but England has different rules about bikes than New York State,
and the Springer, bare to the bones, didn't have turn signals, mirrors, or a baffled exhaust system. I loved it too
much to change a thing, not to mention the money it
would cost to get it over here and do the work, so I kissed
it good-bye.

That was my first big lesson in the sale of custom bikes.
Not everybody is as hog wild, pardon the pun, about your
ideas as you are. What you see as a bold statement, like a
saddle the size of a postage stamp and the thickness of a
slice of bread, the next man, or woman, may see as a very
sore ass. In any case Jess had his own ideas about the bike
he intended to build and several drastic drops in price
could not convince him otherwise.

The officer with the probing hands opens my pocket cau-
tiously, as if I may be wired to explode, and slips his thumb
and index finger inside. Out comes the Bic. I don't hear

the sounds of hammers being cocked and no one is reading me my Miranda rights, so I assume I'm still legal. Then
he takes another dip into the denim and out comes the
real culprit, a chrome object about the size and weight of
a pocket cigar holder.

"What's this?" he asks, with a voice that hints towards
a suspicion of heavy drugs.

"A chrome case," I reply. I could tell him what's in it
but I'm starting to become a bit righteous myself. This guy
is treating me like a class-A felon. On top of that it's starting to rain. On top of that we've still got to get home.

"Don't get smart with me," he retorts.

Suitably chastened, I remain silent as he pops the lid,
looks inside with his flashlight, then still not convinced
that I'm not carrying a syringe and several bags of smack,
tips the contents into his free hand.

I smile victoriously as my tortoise shell reading glasses
hit his palm.

"I needed them to read the wine list at the saloon," I
say, thinking that my ordeal has just ended and I might as
well leave 'em laughing.

He stares at me stone faced.

"Have you been drinking?" he asks.

Oh, shit, I've done it now, I think. "One at dinner," I
answer.

"Stay where you are," he orders.

My stomach sinks.

I move my eyes a bit to my left and see the reason I am
here now, in this rather unfortunate circumstance, with
biceps headed to his patrol car to get the roadside breathalyzer. The reason's name is Tom, but I have tagged him
the Colonel. He's got a face that a mutual friend once
described as a relief map of the Rockies, a drooping Wild
Bill Hickok mustache, and a Camel hanging from his lips.

He looks very relaxed, but then again, he's not about to be breathalyzed. He's also got a camera aimed at me. Anything for a little bit of publicity.

"No pictures," the muscular cop barks as he returns from his vehicle.

The Colonel is responsible for everything, or maybe he's not. It was me, after all, who wrote the book in 1992, a chronicle of my biking adventures, after a rocky reentrance into the world of V-Twins at the age of forty. Titled *Hog Fever*, and based primarily on spending a fortune to turn the Springer into a custom Hog, it found a small but loyal audience in Europe and America. The Colonel was, perhaps, the book's greatest fan—I think he bought six thousand copies—and after tracking me down via my mother, whose address appears on a reprinted letter, written by a Southern lawyer to my family, assuring them that he would keep me out of jail following a bike-related arrest in Georgia in 1965, the Colonel assured me that *Hog Fever* would "have 'em laughin' from coast to coast."

"Just a matter of promotion," promised the P. T. Barnum of biker anthologies.

Well, he sold me.

Six weeks later I paid to have the Springer shipped to his garage in Indianapolis.

"Gotta have the bike to promote the book," he reasoned.

A few months after that, on July 27, he rolled my chromed money pit up a ramp and into the back of a Wells Fargo trailer and hauled it west, to Sturgis, South Dakota. The rest is history, or at least up to this point.

I did have a drink, a margarita, or two, about half an hour ago. I complained that they were light on the tequila. Now I'm praying I was right.

The rain has escalated and we're still about fifty miles

from Rapid City, South Dakota, which during The Sturgis
Rally and Races, or "bike week," was about as close to a
room as we could get to Sturgis. We are riding from Deadwood, another satellite town that has been totally taken
over by the half-million bikers that roar into the Black
Hills every year, and we've just had dinner with Billy Kidd,
former Olympic gold medal ski champion. He's visiting
with his girlfriend and he loves my bike, or so he said
about five hours ago in Sturgis, so we rode over to have
dinner with them and let him take it around the block.

It's amazing who's in Sturgis. From pro wrestlers and
film icons to world class rock 'n' roll bands, playing at the
Hells' Angels' owned Buffalo Chip campground, plus a
busload of young ladies who arrived from Iowa a few hours
ago, all of whom are accomplished lap dancers, and prepared to take over from the last crew who have worn out
their G-strings during the first three days of this seven-
day marathon.

Lap dancing is essentially the art of the wet dream. You
pay a cover charge, which gives you a table and drink, sit
there as the music kicks in and watch as the girls take the
stage, in varying degrees of nudity, usually a G-string and
high heels, although cowboy boots or bare feet are also
favorite accessories. After a few more ten dollar beers, and
a suitable period of ogling the goods, the customer more
or less signals the babe of his choice, which means entic-
ing her to the table with a couple of twenties slipped down
the side of her G-string.

After that, let the good times roll.

She sits in his lap and rubs up against him while he
settles back and pretends that there's not a hundred other
armchair stallions in the same sweaty bar room with the
same sweaty thoughts on their minds. Trying like hell to

keep all hands on deck—don't touch the goods—it's sort of Zen and the art of mental masturbation.

During my one and only visit to Shotgun Willy's—which was to rescue a friend in the throes of divorce who'd mysteriously veered off during a group ride—I arrived in time to witness a guy, who looked like a middle-aged preppie out for a walk on the wild side in his Docksiders, get a bit carried away as he proceeded to unzip his fly in an attempt to reveal his enthusiasm. At which point the siliconed blonde whose G-string he had padded with crisp twenty dollar bills, belted him in the head with a solid right hand, then shouted for assistance. Moments later, the flaccid offender, jeans neatly creased and fly at half-mast, was hoisted from his chair and tossed from the bar, very unceremoniously, by a couple of oversized gentlemen with beards.

"Would you please blow into this, sir," the muscular cop requests.

The last time I was breathalyzed I was living in London, riding down the Embankment on the west side of the River Thames at eleven o'clock on Christmas Eve. I failed the breath test, got hauled to jail, used my one phone call to phone my now ex-wife, explained my situation, and she hung up on me. Merry Christmas.

This time I attempt a few quick breath exercises. A actor friend once tipped me to the fact that you can sometimes beat a breathalyzer by inhaling and exhaling vigorously just before taking the test. I sound like a locomotive by the time the officer shoves the thing under my nose and says, "blow."

This has lost any semblance of a little roadside adventure. If I fail the breath test my bike is gone and so am I, straight off for a night in the lockup, to be followed by a day in court and a serious fine. During bike week the Sturgis Police Department has absolutely zero tolerance for any alcohol or drug abuse. There's a hundred dollar fine for even carrying a roach clip, minus the grass. And here I am blowing my way to a custody arrest.

"Again," he says after my first effort, which would have hardly inflated a condom.

I blow again, giving it the last of one full lung.

Another incredibly tense moment as he checks his gauges. Even the Colonel looks worried, as evidenced by the inch-long ash hanging from the tip of his Camel Light.

"Okay."

Okay what? I wonder.

He eyes me and nods his head. "You passed."

Now, suddenly, the cops feel like my closest friends. I stop myself just before offering a few signed copies of my book, which I know the Colonel has stashed in his saddle bags.

"I'm giving you a warning on that taillight, though," he says as he hands me a pink slip of paper with something scrawled on it.

I take it as if I'm receiving a citation for valor in the line of duty.

After that, it's back on the bikes without even exchanging glances, starting them up and heading into the rainy night at about twenty-five miles an hour. One of the police cars follows us for a few minutes, then trails off as we proceed, trembling with cold and fatigue towards our destination, a good hour away.

Sturgis, there's nothing like it. . . .

A WHITE SPORT COAT

Two years later

I'M ON INTERSTATE 80, JUST EAST OF DAVENPORT, IOWA.
It's a bumpy stretch of two-lane blacktop and I'm doing seventy-five miles an hour, which is nothing for a hundred and ten horsepower engine, pushing a six hundred pound chassis and carrying a hundred and sixty-eight pound man. The bike would go nearly twice this speed if I kicked it into fifth gear and cranked it up, but not at this moment. At this moment, seventy-five miles an hour is close to suicide.

The rain is hitting my face with the sharp force of pellets from an air gun and I'm furiously wiping the left side of my dark glasses with the index finger of my left hand, but my riding gloves are so wet that the reddish brown color has begun to seep from their leather and coat the lens, adding a sepia affect to whatever is left of my vision. My right hand feels as if it has frozen solid and bonded with the throttle; I wonder if I could slow down if I had to.

What am I doing here?

I don't have a choice.

It's sink or swim, or more accurately, ride or fall. There's a big, ugly Mack truck in front of me, throwing back gallons of dirty water, mixed with a hail of gravel, another gray metal monster barreling up my rear end, threatening to crush me while ensuring that I maintain my suicide speed, and a third, an oil tanker, overtaking on the left, whipping up another layer of moisture and oil, like the tailwind of a hurricane.

My boots have two inches of rain inside them, my feet are numb, and my pants are so wet and cold that I'm seriously considering releasing my bladder just to warm things up. Sandwiched in between fifty tons of steel and rubber, I'm wondering if they've checked their mirrors or looked down from their cabs and clocked the lone mariner, like a waterlogged ghost, streaking along the gray ribbon of road to hell knows where.

This morning I was warm and dry in Illinois. Wearing a T-shirt, watching the sun rise in my rearview mirror, and singing an inspired rendition of "A White Sport Coat and A Pink Carnation," a song I never actually liked but for some reason had lodged irrevocably in my brain following a TV ad for a '50s Music Collection—picked up by satellite from last night's motel room.

My helmet was strapped to the bungee cord that was holding my leather jacket to the rear fender of my motorcycle, and my hair was blowing free in the wind. My greatest concern in life was whether the SPF 17 sunscreen would keep my nose from ultraviolet incineration.

I figured I could do six hundred miles before sundown.

Now I'm wondering if I can do six more before my funeral service.

Blame it on Richard Gurling Sears. Or more accurately, on an old black and white photograph of him that I first noticed, sitting in a shroud of dust, on his desk, over forty years ago.

"Is that you, Grandpa?" I asked, staring at a fresh-faced kid sitting on a contraption that looked like a bicycle with a strap-on engine. It was his nose that gave him away. Somewhere between a hawk's beak and a banana, it was a sizable proboscis, even in 1907, when the photo had been taken.

"Yes. Rode a Bat in those days. Thought I was cock of the walk," he answered, his faded gray eyes honing in on mine.

"A Bat?"

"It was a British motorbike. Cost me five quid (about $7.50). Damn fast, too."

Grandpa was about seventy and hadn't lived in England since he was nineteen but he still clipped his words like a Londoner.

I was hooked. "How fast?"

"Fifteen, maybe twenty miles an hour."

"I can peddle a bike that fast," I snickered.

"Not up a hill."

While I pondered that possibility, he took the silver-framed picture down from its perch and rubbed the dust away with a white cotton handkerchief, a permanent accessory to his Harris tweed jacket.

The black Bat shone brightly through the glass.

"Good experience to operate a motorbike. Every young man should know how to operate a motor bicycle," he concluded, placing the photo back in a more prominent position on the mantle above his desk.

———

This is crazy.

The rain has escalated to flood conditions and I can barely see the highway. I'm literally following the taillights of the truck in front of me, locked on like a heat-seeking missile. I've given up wiping my sunglasses, they're fogged and dripping, so I've pulled them down so I can just peek out over the top of their rounded lenses. Of course that means my eyeballs are bare and the water pellets have a clean shot at them, so I keep closing them, then opening them again, sometimes one at a time, sometimes both, which means I'm sloshing down the highway with my eyes shut. On top of this, I can't swallow, which for some reason, maybe because of the dirt and gravel in my mouth, or lack of saliva due to adrenaline secretion, I need to do every thirty seconds. The reason I can't swallow is that the strap of my helmet has loosened just enough for it to catch the head wind and plane upward from my forehead, causing the nylon to dig inward against my windpipe like a garrote.

I'm being strangled.

The only way I can counter this attack is by releasing my left hand from the handlebars and using it to press down against the top of the helmet, thus easing the pressure on my throat, enough so that I am able to gulp down whatever it is that is lodged in the back of my mouth. It also means that I am traveling with my eyes shut and only one hand on the bars, except during the alternate intervals in which I'm choking while peering out over the top of the filthy lenses of the dark glasses.

It's during one of these seeing but not breathing spells that I spot something in the distance that gives me a ray of hope. An underpass, like a concrete oasis, where the interstate intersects and travels beneath another road. Shelter. It looks like heaven to me.

Now all I have to do is steer the motorcycle onto the hard shoulder and make it stop beneath the archway. I do this by turning on the right indicator and pumping gently on the front brake as I attempt to glide gracefully off the highway and out from under the grill of the truck behind. I'm rewarded with what feels like a hundred gallons of cold water over my right side as the insensitive bastard splashes by.

By the time grandpa had joined the U.S. Army for the start of W.W. I, he was already bald. Not only bald, but devoid of all body hair, a result of a nervous disorder he'd suffered in his late teens. He did wear a hairpiece, but in those days, before the magic of Hair Club for Men, toupees or wigs tended to resemble badly woven bird's nests. His reddish-brown thatch never sat quite right, and according to the speed at which he moved, or the velocity of the wind, it could adopt some fantastic angles, giving him a decidedly off-kilter appearance, as if his face and the top of his head were not quite connected. On that blustering day in late November, his hair was balanced at about a thirty degree angle. Listing like a ship at sea, before he righted it with a swipe from his left hand as we hopped into his Ford Fairlane 500 and drove to the outskirts of Easton, Pennsylvania, to the warehouse of his heavy machinery business.

It was my sixteenth birthday.

We parked in the lot, got out of the car and walked silently toward the huge white door of the faded green building.

I sensed that something major was about to transpire.

Once at the building, grandpa pressed a button on the side of the wall and an old electric motor groaned as the door rose with the sound of breaking thunder.

It took my eyes a few seconds to adjust to the dim light inside.

"Happy birthday," he said.

It was sitting dead center of the concrete floor, circled by air compressors, coiled hoses, loose wrenches, and hydraulic lifts. Cast in backlight as the autumn sun poked holes through the grit and grease that smeared the windows along the highway side of the building.

My first impression was of a red and white breadbox, connected by a floorboard to a metal shield and a set of short, flat handlebars. The whole thing was balanced on two small, fat tires.

The words Cushman Golden Eagle were spelled out in dull chrome script and mounted on the side of the squared rear section, below the flat plastic-covered saddle.

I was speechless. The motor scooter looked like a kid's toy, but blown up to sixteen-year-old size. I couldn't wait to climb on.

"You can learn to ride on this machine," proclaimed the former owner of the British Bat.

And I knew my life had been suddenly and irrevocably changed.

I see the deserted bike as I roll out of the rain and continue beneath the archway.

It's a black Harley Sportster, dripping wet and loaded down with a bedroll, camping gear, saddlebags and a windshield. Pushed off the road like a tired mule.

At first I don't see the rider but as my body stops trembling and my eyes adjust to the darkness beneath the bridge I can make out a thin figure, encased in a dark rainsuit and hunched against the concrete wall at the back of the underpass, staring out, forlorn, at the trucks and cars that whiz past at what appears to be impossible speeds, throwing more buckets of dirty water over both our bikes.

He looks over at me and shakes his head in utter disgust.

It's the first time I have a clear view of his face, which is furrowed with deep lines and frowning. His thin red hair is soaked and plastered tight to his mostly bald head and his small brown eyes look like they've seen many miles.

My first thought is, *He's even older than I am,* which seems, somehow, reassuring. Followed by *At least I'm not in this mess on my own,* as I watch him slide down from his perch and walk towards me. Pulling a pack of Marlboros from the inside pocket of his rainsuit, and smacking the bottom against the heel of his hand, he extends a cigarette. I don't smoke but in this case I almost wish I did, as if it would confirm the bond between us.

I decline the cigarette with a shake of my head.

"Last time something like this happened to me I was under one of these things for six and a half hours," he says in a low, nasal voice, void of hope, while surveying the jagged curvature of the low cement ceiling above our heads.

"Maybe it will pass," I answer, attempting an optimism that my feet, now experiencing a strange tingling sensation in the toes, don't share.

"Don't know about that," he counters, as a line of cars rumble ominously across the road above and a stream of trucks continue in a steady hissing procession about ten feet from where we stand.

"There's flooding up the road," he adds, swiping a sodden match over and over again against the abrasive edge of a small metal box. Finally it catches and he lights up the cigarette, continuing to speak with it dangling from his lips. "No rain for six weeks and now a flood. Shit happens."

"Yeah, well . . ." I want to say more, to contribute some appropriate bit of biker philosophy, but I'm stuck on the idea of spending the next six and a half hours inside this hell hole, waiting for one of the hissing ten-tonners, with an amphetamine crazed jockey at the wheel, to career off the road and pulverize us into one screaming heap of steel, teeth, blood, and flesh.

"Where you headed?" I ask, trying to lighten my thoughts.

"Sturgis," he answers.

"Me, too."

He turns toward my motorcycle as if he's assessing its ability to make the journey.

"What kind of bike is that, anyway?"

I follow his eyes.

Other than the basic V-Twin configuration of the engine, it's hard to tell. Beneath all the dirt and road grease, it could be just about anything.

"It's a Big Dog," I answer.

"A what?"

"It was made by a company in Wichita, Kansas," I explain.

"Good looking machine," he replies as he douses the Marlboro in one of the many puddles that decorate the surface beneath our feet. "Too bad it doesn't have a windshield. Must be tough to ride in this weather without one."

I'm suddenly aware of what feels like bullet holes in the skin above my mouth, caused by the rain pelting my face, look over at the bike and recall the exact moment that I turned down the offer of a windshield.

It was a Sunday afternoon in mid-July. We'd had no rain for three weeks. The sky was clear and blue and there was just the hint of a salty breeze coming up from the bay, enough to take the edge off the blazing sun. I was wearing swimming trunks, sipping an icy margarita and standing on the waterside deck of my former house. Talking to Nick Messer, the gravel voiced president of Big Dog Motorcycles, on the telephone. He had called to see what options I wanted on the bike before they shipped it from Kansas.

Saddlebags were my single request.

"And a windshield," he added, as if that was taken for granted.

"I don't think so. I like to feel the wind in my face," I replied, letting the Cointreau sweetened tequila settle luxuriously against my better judgment.

There was a moment of silence in Kansas.

"No windshield," I reconfirmed.

"No windshield." His voice echoed my words, minus the confidence.

I look at the black Sportster, its windshield battened down tight against the storm, then at my new friend's full face helmet—with visor—and at his rubber boots and rainsuit.

I feel naked, cold, and shivering. My boots squish loudly as I shift position, trying to affect a more confident stance.

"You get used to it," I answer, but my voice is nearly swallowed by the belch of air brakes from a passing truck.

He looks quickly at the highway, watches the truck shimmy then regain control, looks at my bike, which appears bare and vulnerable, then back at me, saying, "if we don't get going, we'll never get there."

His statement is simple, but at this precise moment, it seems to hold great and ancient wisdom.

"You're right," I agree.

He anchors his helmet to his head, pulls down the visor, pulls up his riding gloves and straddles his machine. "See you up the road," he says.

His Sportster starts with a confident blast from the straight pipes. A few seconds later he has joined the hiss of the highway.

I watch until his taillight becomes a speck in the distance, feeling vaguely abandoned and wondering if I will ever actually see the nameless rider again.

Then I turn, walk back into the shadows and attempt something that I've been dying to do since I arrived. Urinate. But I can't find it. In England, where my life was lived underwater for twenty years and the chill invaded the bones, the condition is referred to as "dispatch rider's dick." Many a leathered sufferer has been shamed at the public urinal by a shriveled and noncompliant organ. Mine, I believe, has receded into a state of permanent protest and requires considerable coaxing to appear and function. Even then the dismal trickle nowhere near matches the torrents that are threatening beyond the underpass.

Finally, mission accomplished, I turn and address the Big Dog.

"Why the hell am I doing this?"

DAY ONE

IF YOU WISH TO DROWN, DO NOT TORTURE
YOURSELF WITH SHALLOW WATER.

—BULGARIAN PROVERB

THE RAZOR'S EDGE

THREE WEEKS AGO, WHILE ENGAGED IN AN UPHILL EXERCISE ride on my newly acquired mountain bike, I tore the cartilage on the medial side of my right knee. I know this because I've done it before, twice. The immediate physical symptoms are swelling and pain. Sometimes, if I pivot or move in the wrong direction, it feels like someone has just rammed the point of a sharp knife into the side of my knee. I'm hoping that the torn piece doesn't break loose and lock the joint. I may be up and running one minute, down and writhing in agony the next. Hardly a confidence builder, particularly for a man on the road.

Two weeks ago, I was hovering outside the doorway of the bathroom, silently reciting the section of the Lord's prayer that goes, "thy will be done" while my wife performed the "guaranteed ninety-nine percent accurate" version of the home pregnancy test. Watching in slow motion as she turned and said, "well, you've done it again."

Almost fifty-four years old and another baby on the way. My first, Jack, is barely two-and-a-half and I'm already contemplating whether I'll be arriving at his high school graduation on a motorcycle or a walker.

On the tail of the pregnancy alert came the news that the house we were "house-sitting" for friends had been sold. Making us temporarily homeless, and homeless in the Hamptons during the month of August is bad news. Being a summer resort, a hundred miles east of New York City, with world-class ocean beaches and thousand-dollar-a-day home rentals, if you ain't got a place to stay in August, you're out of luck. We were about to become a family of gypsies.

On top of all this, there was my mind.

A delicate piece of machinery at the best of times, it had begun, in a technical sense, to malfunction. Stall would be a more accurate word. I earn my living as a writer and my condition is commonly known as "writer's block." Equivalent to mental constipation. You sit and sit and nothing happens. I couldn't seem to get beyond the first page of anything. Desperate for a new novel, something that was both innovative and inspired, I spent hours staring at the blank blue screen of my word processor. Occasionally I wrote a sentence, sometimes a paragraph, but more often than not my gaze would wander out the window of my office, scanning the road and listening to the distant rumble of motorcycles, cruising Highway 27 en route to Montauk Point. After a therapeutic spell, and suitably titillated by the thumping lullaby, I'd open a drawer and lift out the March '99 issue of *Easyriders* magazine. So well-thumbed that it would just about open by itself to page 99 and a pictorial layout titled "The Razor's Edge". The Edge, in fact, was a silver motorcycle that I had designed from the frame up, building it by faxed drawings, Polaroids and fly-in visits to Wichita, Kansas, for close to a year. A bare to the bones custom motorcycle, it was simplicity itself. Well, simplicity to the tune of twenty-five thousand dollars. Building custom motorcycles, or, more accurately, having them built for you, is an expensive hobby. On top of my writer's block, came my separation anxiety, because after The Edge's first incarnation, I'd brought it home, spent a summer riding it, then shipped it back to Wichita for some necessary alterations.

I was missing it like crazy.

At any hint of my wife's footsteps, *Easyriders* would be closed and jammed back into the drawer and my fingers hastily replaced on the keyboard beneath the blank blue screen.

"How's it going?" She would ask hopefully, her words tightening the pressure lid on my brain.

"Slow," I'd sizzle, frowning as if anxious to get back to the rigors of creation, with no time for small talk.

At the height of these multiple dilemmas, came the telephone call from Big Dog.

"Your bike will be finished in a week."

The Razor's Edge, the Zen Sled, the pinup on page 99, minus the accompanying babe, was ready to come back home. The problem was that being a man of no fixed address, there was no home.

In the midst of this chaos the idea hit.

Sturgis, there's nothing like it.

So with no place to live, a new wife and child, another baby on the way, a blank screen, a teetering bank balance, a twenty-five thousand dollar motorcycle ready for delivery and a mind that felt parboiled, I made my decision. Escape. Out of the armchair and into the saddle.

On the road.

Fantasy and reality occasionally collide.

It's three A.M. and I can't sleep.

My pregnant wife and my son Jack have gone. Departed yesterday for Greece, to the home of her mother and step-father. It's the first time since Jack was born that we've been apart and I feel a hollow in my heart. I miss them like crazy.

My knee hurts like hell.

So does the truth: I've never done a cross-country mo-torcycle ride on my own.

Scenes of accidents and amputations flash through my head like the disjointed frames of a cheap horror film.

I may never see my family again.

It's a long haul from Amagansett, New York, to Sturgis, South Dakota. About 2,000 miles, probably more like 2,500 if I take the northern route through Canada. Also, I tend to lose my way. As my father, who regularly got lost in the same town we'd lived in for twenty years, once told me, "It's a family failing."

Head-wise, it's an entirely different reality.

Sturgis, nestled in the beautiful rolling Black Hills, is a small town generally populated by 10,000 ordinary folks. During bike week, however, things change. For over sixty years—since the Jackpine Gypsies hosted the first Rally and Races in 1938—the beginning of August has been devoted to motorcycles. Now, between 350,000 and 500,000 riders and enthusiasts descend on Sturgis—along with the surrounding towns of Rapid City, Deadwood, Spearfish, and Custer. The locals flee, renting their houses, front lawns, store spaces, motels, derelict school buses—anything that can accommodate a human body. And Sturgis is transformed. Tattoo studios, knife dealers, and strip clubs spring up where there were once shops sell-ing baby powder and diapers. Tents are pitched on front lawns, hammocks hung and campsites erected. Rock bands roll into town, headed for the Buffalo Chip campground. World Championship wrestlers take their corners at a special site, located a few blocks from the ambulance station on Sherman Street.

Every American motorcycle and parts manufacturer worth their salt has a marquee in Sturgis.

Every outlaw biker club flies its colors.

Main Street is a twenty-four-hour parade on steel horses.

Shoulder to shoulder, biceps to biceps, armpit to armpit, tattoo to tattoo, and camshaft to exhaust pipe, the roar never ends.

Depending upon your horsepower and level of self-confidence, Sturgis can be a very intimidating place.

Lying here now, contemplating the distance between myself and this tiny explosion on the map, while figuring that I need to cover about five hundred miles a day to get there at the height of the rally, I go through an inventory of my own insecurities.

It's hardly a trip around the world, but it is a long haul. What if the motorcycle breaks down? I'm no mechanic. What if it rains the whole way there? I hate riding on slick roads. What if I crash? What if my knee seizes up while I'm fighting for my life with a gang of bike thieves? What if I never think of an idea for another book?

What if?

PACKING

EVERYTHING I'M TAKING IS CRUSHED INTO TWO SADDLEBAGS, each approximately the size of the case I usually carry my personal computer in.

On previous road trips, before common sense overcame vanity (the bike does look better without saddlebags), I traveled light. Socks, underpants, and toothbrush stuffed down the front of my leather trousers, running from my crotch halfway to my knee. Hung like a donkey to begin with, my prodigious size diminished daily as I kept tossing wet and dirty socks out and replacing them from the fabric of my cotton leg warmer. By the end of the ride I was a certified castrato.

This time I had room for a road map, a leather jacket, a rainsuit, socks, T-shirts, underwear, and scarves to protect my face. Also a pair of jeans. Then there's my shaving kit, and my tools, including a miniature halogen flashlight, a Timberline knife, an eight-in-one screwdriver, two rolls of duct tape, and a set of ratchets. Enough to bang the bottom of the carburetor if the float sticks, or to be able to tape a loose ignition wire.

I'm going to travel in a T-shirt and a pair of bombachas, which are Argentinean gaucho (cowboy) pants. They look a little like stylized combat fatigues: khaki-colored, roomy in the thigh, while tapering at the calf to a buttoned cuff, but the real selling point is that they are wide enough in the knee to accommodate my new orthopedic support bandage.

And my Spanish leather cowboy boots. To date this pair have had five resoles and the left has a permanent scar on its toe, from kicking up against the gear levers of my previous motorcycles. They look tired and beat, but they fit like gloves and I feel they're lucky, as opposed to a similar pair, in black, that I was wearing on my last cross-country attempt. They required a surgical removal following a freak accident that ended my ride and nearly my right foot.

All this stuff is running through my mind like a runaway express.

Toward sunrise my one desire is to throw a power switch to my brain and shut the whole thing off. Instead, I keep checking the luminous dial on the bedside radio, then, lurching upwards in a semi–sit up, I crane my neck to search the sky through the curtained window. *Clouds. No clouds. Clouds. Please, no rain.*

All the time telling myself that even if I get to sleep now, I'll only get a couple of hours, so I settle back against the mattress, pull the pillow down over my eyes, and continue to watch home disaster movies on the back of my lids.

Morning comes and I'm fried. The last thing I feel capable of is a ride to Buffalo, New York, up by Niagara Falls on the Canadian border, and over five hundred miles from East Hampton. A shower doesn't make me feel much better so I dress in my orthopedic support bandage—

with a whole cut in the knee for purposes, I believe, of ventilation—then pull on my bombachas, T-shirt, and boots before limping into the kitchen.

I fire up the stove and put on the kettle, in preparation for mate. It's a herbal green tea from Argentina (pronounced mateh), which comes in kilo bags and smells like grass. The correct way to drink it is to fill a specially hollowed gourd with the dried leaves, soak them with hot water (not boiling) then sip the bitter brew through a metal straw, called a bombilla (sounds like bombisha). The buzz, after a few minutes of soaking and slurping, is like a triple shot of espresso, or a single line of cocaine (if my rock 'n' roll recall is correct).

By the time I've sucked the gourd dry I'm not even limping. Sturgis? It's a sprint down the road.

I can't wait to ride.

TEST RIDER

THE BIKE IS ON LOAN. I'd never even seen it till last night, when it arrived in the back of a pickup truck, driven by Mike from Biker's Dream, looking like a baby Brahma with a flash paint job.

My first reaction, after climbing into the saddle, was that I was riding high. Too high. I'm used to chopped down, lowered bikes that give me the feeling that, if necessary, I could always slide off and continue my journey by foot—a mistake that has proved, at least once, nearly fatal. The low-slung effect is achieved only by serious compromises to the suspension systems. In other words, get rid of the springs, avoid all potholes and pack a tube of Anusol and a kidney belt for any distance over fifty miles.

As I examine the Big Dog now, in the glow cast by the bare bulb of the overhead light in the garage, it looks strong, solid, and roadworthy. Like it wants to travel. The five gallon tank is adorned with subtle purple flames, streaking through the black lacquered paint.

It is not, however, what I'd call a lean machine. More a quarterhorse, this bike is about function. It has fat, heavy-duty shock absorbers, large handlebar-mounted gauges, a belt drive, and a well-cushioned saddle, contoured to hug tight to its frame. It also has a T.P. (Total Performance) 107 cubic inch engine, or about 1750 cc's, like a small car, set on rubber mounts, to ensure that I don't rattle the fillings in my teeth as I hurtle towards South Dakota.

Then there's the console, sitting on top of the tank. I've never seen one like it, but that's what makes bikes so interesting. Personality. In this case, the console looks as if it's made of Lucite, or Plexiglas. In other words, you can see straight through it, right down and into the maze of wires that are attached to a squared electronic device that bears a disturbing resemblance to a time bomb. This bit of advanced technology is actually an onboard computer, an electronics module, that will record and store everything that I do and don't do to the bike: top speeds, r.p.m.s during blast-offs from traffic lights, low-end performance, sweat on the handgrips, tears on the saddle. All will be revealed and analyzed back at headquarters, in Wichita.

The Big Dog has everything.

Everything, that is, except a windshield.

It's packed and full of gas.

I'm wailing behind a full gourd of mate.

The garage door is open and my bombachas are flapping in the morning breeze. It's showtime.

"You know, you're doing this for all of us."

The voice is a sweet whisper, and comes from behind me.

I turn to see Jennie, the owner of the house, walking down the stone front steps, camera in hand.

Doing this for all of us? What exactly does she mean by that? Paranoia kicks in. I know I've become a bit of an inconvenience lately. A spare part in the midst of moving mayhem.

I turn and meet her eyes. There is no malice in them, no cynicism.

But, doing it for all of us? I'm not exactly going off to war, to save the world.

I look again. Now I know what it is that I see. I see someone who is trapped. I recognize the look because I've seen it in the mirror, at different times, in my own eyes. For Jennie, I know it will pass, but right now, with her life packed in cardboard boxes and the week ahead devoted to rummaging through piles of clothes, saying good-byes, knowing that she won't be back to this place, not in the same way, ever again, and knowing what lies ahead— unpacking, rebuilding, reordering her life, I understand her feelings. She is trapped, inside this moment of turmoil and sadness.

But so am I.

I have boxed myself into this trip. My family is gone. I've got no place to live for a month. I've borrowed a motorcycle. I'm expected in Sturgis.

Like it or not I'm going.

Maybe Jennie doesn't see it, but we are both caught by circumstance, by time, by who we are and what we are.

You're doing this for all of us.

I can see the reflection in her eyes. To her, the bike looks like freedom.

"Well, get on with it then!"

My insight is shattered by Peter's voice as he walks down the steps. Peter's the pragmatist. No messing around, he cuts to the quick.

"Right," I answer, then start the motorcycle.

Time is moving again, away from the feelings of sadness, away from knowing that when I come back my friends will be gone. Away from the knowledge that everything changes, like it or not.

"See you in France," I say.

She snaps a picture and freezes the moment forever.

Then I'm gone.

STRAY COINS

IS IT ME, OR IS IT THE MOTORCYCLE? Everything seems to be rattling. I'm not even a mile from the house and all I can think about is what's falling off. Is my leather jacket secured to the rear of the saddle, will the bungee cords hold up at high speed? Are the saddlebags securely fastened? Will the plastic garbage bags that I've used to line the leather saddlebags keep the rain off my underwear? What rain? Is the Timberline knife vibrating out from the top of my boot? Is that sound, like stray coins in a washing machine, coming from underneath the engine?

I turn right, heading for a shortcut to rejoin 27 West toward New York City, across a section of railroad tracks. The vibration of the tracks beneath the wheels causes the clanking sound beneath the engine to increase. Now it sounds like coins in a beer can. No, this can't be normal. Something has broken loose. I ransack my limited mechanical brain for possibilities. The bike's still moving so it's nothing major. But it's loud, and getting louder. Now what? Turn around? After such a ceremonial exit, resplendent with watery eyes and heroic feelings, it would be far too humiliating to rattle back into the driveway and call for help. I should just pull over, stop the bike, get off, and take a look. But even that seems unacceptable, as if to stop after one mile would somehow and irrevocably destroy the momentum of my undertaking. That followed by an image of myself, stranded on a remote road in the middle of nowhere, with the Big Dog's engine in pieces at my feet.

Not a pretty sight.

I pull over onto a verge of green grass, stop the bike, climb off, and bend down beside it. At first I don't see anything unusual, but as my mind settles and clears, allowing my eyes to focus without the fear that this could be a major setback to my journey, I notice a circular metal dishlike object attached to two black wires. The object is perforated and appears wedged between the frame and the right rear foot peg. I reach forward and take hold of it.

It's the horn.

I consider tearing it away from the wires and sticking it inside one of the saddlebags. Or, I could tape it to the frame, a roadside repair that even I am capable of making, but what if it shakes loose again and interferes with some more vital part of the engine.

It's only a horn.

I can just about recall the number of times I've used a horn while riding. Hardly ever. Still, it would be proper etiquette to arrive at Big Dog with their bike intact. There are also a couple of other considerations. The first is I'd like to be as legal as possible, and a horn is required in every state, not that I envision a roadside "horn check," but anything's possible. As it stands I'm riding a bike that is not registered to me. In fact, since the Big Dog turned up without license plates I slapped on one of my own, intending to remove it in Sturgis and attach it to my new bike. That's illegal. Also, I don't have a U.S. motorcycle license, too busy, or lazy, to make the forty minute drive to Riverhead to take the test. So I'm traveling with a British license, a thing about the size of phone book, although substantially thinner, and folded into a plastic envelope. Since I'm a U.S. citizen and resident, having not lived in England in over three years, technically I don't have a license at all. I can't even fake a decent British accent.

Suddenly ripping the horn off and tossing into a saddlebag seems like a bad idea.

I stand up and look around. I'm just over the tracks on Abraham's Path and only a few minutes from Paul's house. Paul is a biker. Leathered, visored, and riding in the middle of the coldest winter, he's also a mechanic and he's looked after my succession of nonstarters since I moved here in '96. "You break down at 3 A.M., call me, I'll come out and get you, no problem," he has always promised.

I get back on the bike, start it up, and rattle to his house.

Even this minor diversion has the feeling of defeat about it. Obviously, I'm behind schedule, although until now, I didn't realize I was on such a tight deadline. Fuck Paul, maybe I need a shrink.

He is standing in his driveway, a tall, dark, wiry thirty-year old, bent down beside the engine of a black Kawasaki Ninja. At a hundred and sixty miles per hour out of the box the Ninja and Paul were a match made in heaven. The last time I saw them together he was on top of it, going like hell, doing a wheelie down Route 27 in front of Cyril's Fish House restaurant. I was sipping a Corona and there was a cop sitting on the stool next to me, but by the time he'd stood up, as if to make sure what he'd seen was real, Paul was half way to the Montauk lighthouse.

He takes his vacations at motorcycle racing schools.

The Speed King greets me with a large, wrenchlike handshake and an inquisitive look at both my bike and packed saddlebags.

I say, "Sturgis."

The single word seems to explain everything.

"No windshield. You're bad," he comments.

That's a compliment, coming from the Terror of Route 27, but before I can take a bow, he asks, "are you riding the Taconic Parkway north?"

"I was thinking of the Thruway to Albany," I answer, although, at this point, my route is still rather vague in my mind.

"No, you want the Taconic. It's a better ride. Trust me, I did it last weekend. You don't want the Thruway. It's loaded with trucks."

I'm looking at his bike and still thinking about his wheelie, only half listening to his directions as I slip in the news about the broken horn.

Half an hour later, he removes his welding goggles and says, "that bracket will last longer than you will."

An encouraging thought.

After that, the rattling is confined to my mind, as I roll out of East Hampton, wondering just what Paul really said regarding the route to the Taconic Parkway and if I should risk trying to find it.

It takes me about an hour and a half to make it from the multimillion-dollar homes, smooth roads, manicured lawns and roadside cappuccino parlors of the Hamptons to the backbreaking asphalt craters of Route 112, with its multiplex cinemas and multiple McDonald's, en route to Port Jefferson. I can already feel myself shaping up to match the demands of my changing environment. Everything seems tougher and more real, from the rough highway to the malls, to the faces of the people that I pass. The baseball hat and designer sunglasses (the official Hamptons uniform) quotient has dropped from 1 in 1, to 1 in 200. And there aren't many Mercedes SUVs (official Hamptons vehicle), let alone Hummers.

Once in Port Jefferson, I park the bike in a line for the boat and grab a cup of coffee at a portside bar. Already I'm becoming an observer. Listening in on conversations and studying faces. Trying not to be too obvious while hiding behind the dark lenses of my sunglasses.

I haven't been alone in a while and the solitary feeling brings back ghosts from my past. In the early seventies, after being disenrolled from the Marine Corps Officer Training Program, I hit the road for Mexico and did not reappear for a year. By then I was draped in a blanket that doubled as a sleeping bag, had given away my shoes—influenced by a vegetarian commune in San Francisco—was dressed in my only pair of jeans which were held together by an elaborate quilt of patches, and carried a guitar in place of an M-14, along with a wide variety of hallucinogens which had lodged irrevocably in my cerebral hemispheres.

While my friends were attending graduate schools, coming home from Vietnam in body bags, starting families, or beginning careers, I was sleeping under railway trestles. Psychedelic drugs reigned as instant enlightenment and I demanded the full awakening.

Now, thirty years later, as I ride the bike into the cargo hold of the ferry and watch as two blue shirts tie it down, I've got that feeling again, as if I am opening myself up to something new and vast. It's a feeling that defies age, sort of frightening but also beckoning, like something I have to do, although I'm not exactly certain why I need it now.

When I began riding, almost forty years ago, on the Cushman Golden Eagle, there were no helmet laws. There were still no laws when I graduated to a Norton, and I got hooked on the feeling of the wind in my hair and the freedom of sound and vision that a bare head allows. When the laws came into effect I initially felt less secure with a helmet on than without one, less aware of my world and certainly restricted in mobility, as if I had suddenly been sentenced to wearing a fishbowl on top of my shoulders, causing me to be one step removed from the sounds of the road and the sights to either side. Since then I have read numerous studies and safety comparisons between wearing a helmet and not wearing one. Incidents, following an accident, of being strangled by the strap, of suffering a broken neck while some well-meaning samaritan attempts to remove the helmet, and a long list of reports of helmets shattering on impact, as the materials used to construct them—certified by the Department of Transportation—are generally tested at only a fraction of the speed of an actual collision.

I also have friends who swear that their lives have been saved by a helmet.

It's a personal decision and, for me, the heightened awareness of hearing clearly and the advantage of peripheral vision, coupled with the mobility of my neck and shoulders, tips the scales.

On the Connecticut side of the Long Island Sound, with the bike out and me on it, the helmet secured by bungie cord to the frame—no helmet laws in Connecticut—I'm sitting in the parking lot looking up at the steady stream of cars and trucks that pass over the bridge forming a section of Interstate 95, almost directly above my head. I rack my brains for Paul's directions but it seems they have been left in another more tranquil frame of reality, as opposed to this nightmare of air brakes and horns.

A detour sign, two doubtful turns, a few curses, and I'm there, stuck inside the nightmare, looking back down at where I came from, at the parking lot, the Sound and the ferryboat. Wondering where I went wrong.

It takes a roadside stop, a map check, and a friendly gas station attendant to turn me around and head me in the opposite direction, towards Ossining, where I am assured I'll link up with the Taconic Parkway.

I've forgotten what Interstate traffic is like, particularly around cities where roads converge and arteries clog, but now I'm there, shoulder to axle, knee to bumper, mouth to exhaust pipe, like a clot in the vein. Breathing in the stink of hot rubber and unleaded gas, while my bare head and unmuffled ears are assailed by the sounds of squealing tires, air brakes, and blaring horns. Crawling over an unfinished patch of highway, my wardrobe, tools, and cell phone bumping up and down on the back fender, hoping I don't lose anything, and wondering how I'd pick it up if I did, all the while locked in on either side by agitated commuters and long distance truckers.

Feeling a bit insecure.

I eat a grain or two of fresh gravel as I scrape by the side of a rusted Jeep Wagoneer, its driver casting an admiring glance at the Big Dog, then at me, with eyes that say, *Nice bike. You lucky bastard.*

At the moment, I'd trade him even on the Wagoneer and a three mile ride home.

Finally, traffic thins and I'm going sixty. Concentrating on road signs, determined not to miss Route 9 to Ossining. The rattles, internal and external, have nearly stopped as my mind firms up by virtue of sheer concentration.

One stop to put on my helmet as I recross the New York State line. Standing by the side of the road I'm nearly blown over by the side winds and backdrafts created by the passing trucks. From a standing perspective it looks fast, loud, and dangerous out there. The Big Dog looks surprisingly tame, idling quietly on the shoulder. All that changes once I'm back in the saddle, twisting the throttle open and flying like a bullet, right past the same trucks that spit dirt on me three minutes ago.

Finally there's the sign for Ossining, followed by another for the Taconic Parkway and I begin to feel better.

The Taconic looks like the yellow brick road. Thank you, Paul. Hello, Sturgis, I'm on my way, with the new silver bike dangling like a carrot in front of my nose.

The silver bike.

It will not be my first silver bike. I saw my first thirty-five years ago, sitting with a FOR SALE sign on it by the side of the road in Sea Girt, New Jersey. It was a clear, hot day in late August and I was an eighteen-year-old lifeguard, out for a top-down cruise in my '57 Ford convertible. The Norton Electra stopped me dead. It stood out against the backdrop of sand, white-painted woodsided houses, and gray-green ocean like an archetypal symbol, carved in metal against the sky. It was a million fantasies made real. Wild times and fast rides. Outlaws and sex. It was completion. I had to touch it, sit on it. Ride it.

Four hundred dollars later, I did. Wobbling across the Bay bridge that connected Sea Girt to Point Pleasant Beach and the family's shore cottage. Frightened that the beast would run away with me on its back, I never shifted out of second gear, bumping along at twenty miles an hour for the entire three miles to my door. Climbing off as if I had just scaled Everest. It was my first ride on a real motorcycle.

A month later I had a black beret, longer hair, wrap-around shades and my first pair of engineer boots.

When September came, and the shore emptied, I rode the Norton back home to Philadelphia.

Seventy miles along Route 70 west. Whipping along at sixty-five, bouncing up and down against the long hard saddle and feeling every joint in the surface of the road. Conscious of everything from the wind in my face, threatening to lift my beret and rip off my sunglasses, to the smells of pine needles and grass, dried from a summer drought and blowing past me. Me and the silver bike, joined at the hip, with time dissolving all around us. Feeling, for the first time, that I'd found the center of the universe.

JOHN

THIRTY-FIVE YEARS LATER, TWO LANES OF SMOOTH TARMAC
lead through a tunnel of green trees, gently banking
through acres of virgin countryside, as I travel towards
another silver bike. I'm rolling. My paranoia is shutting
down a piece at a time and as it does my senses are opening. Suddenly the air smells of perfume: pine, grass and
pure earth, all mixed and fuel injected up my nostrils. I'm
beginning to relax. I can tell because the Big Dog has
begun to feel almost pliable between my legs, as if it's
made of flesh and bone, moving and shifting with my
body. Its sound is low and throaty, and I can barely feel
it vibrate.

The road travels across miles and miles of small rolling
hills with deep forest to my right and mountains and valleys to my left.

Everything is now. The smell of the air, the canopy of
blue sky, the heat of the sun on my neck, the wind in my
face, the roar of the bike, the sensation of speed.

Not a car in front of me, or a car behind.

Then, maybe because a few miles back I saw a cut-off

sign for Waterbury, his old hometown, or perhaps by some deeper intuition, I think of my old riding buddy, John. More than thought, it's the sensation of his presence.

I look to my left and can imagine him there, riding close to me, his long, sandy brown hair blowing behind him, with that smile on his face, that look that says that this is it, as good as it gets. His motorcycle, a road-worn Harley Electraglide, is purring, keeping up easily with mine. We haven't ridden together in a long time and I had almost forgotten how well he handles his bike, like he's morphed from the saddle, wearing a gray T-shirt, a pair of jeans, and his beat-up engineer boots. The same clothes he was wearing the last time I saw him.

Leave it to John to make this run with me. He loved Sturgis, with its outlaws and campgrounds, rock bands, and parties. But more than that he loved to ride.

I met him at a party in a New York City restaurant. It was a going away party for the Bridge Club, a group of industry and media icons who met up every so often for a cross-country motorcycle extravaganza, complete with traveling wine cellar. Their name came from their first run together, from the Brooklyn Bridge in New York to the San Francisco Bay Bridge in California.

I was at the party because I knew one of the original members and had always wanted to ride cross-country. For me, the party was awkward. Coats, ties, high-polished shoes, and short, well-groomed hair, but not me. I was wearing a T-shirt, jeans, and hair half-way down my back. I knew only one other person in the room and felt as if I was about to be discovered as a gate-crasher and asked to leave. Generally not at a loss for words, it was as if my volume control had been switched to mute. At about that time I spotted John. He was different. Not only his casual dress and long hair but the look in his eyes, a quick sparkle, a certain glint that said he wasn't taking anything too seriously. Just having a good time, he didn't appear to need a thing. He looked ready for the road.

Who is that guy? I wondered, but amidst the wine and celebratory toasts I never had a chance to find out.

Once underway, following a shotgun exit from Manhattan, including a few wrong turns and the loss of my rear brake, he truly became an enigma. By no means on the fastest bike, he still seemed to turn up miles ahead of me, and in the strangest places.

I'd be bouncing along on my stretched and severely lowered Softail, cursing the day I let the Battistini brothers alter the frame and wondering if I had, once again, managed to fall behind the club's chase truck—my only hope of rescue, not to mention a drink—when he'd appear, stepping out from a thicket of trees, surrounded by a halo of smoke. Snapping pictures.

I'd fake a panoramic smile, aim my wind chiseled features directly ahead, accelerate and blast on by, only to be caught by him a few minutes later, riding his big Glide like he was in an easy chair. He'd nod in my direction and pass on by. At which point I'd check my speedometer—80—and wonder how fast he was traveling and how the hell he made it look like slow motion. Was he stoned or was it me?

Then I wouldn't see him till evening, when we all gathered round the dinner table, sipping vintage wine. By then I was too tired to communicate.

By the second day, already five hundred miles closer to Las Vegas (our destination) and not having had any deep or revelatory conversations with the rest of the pack I was even more curious. The snapper seemed to travel alone, either ahead of everyone else or purposefully behind, but more often than not he'd be in hiding, with his camera and something that looked suspiciously like a small pipe.

It was after a tight corner in the Blue Ridge Mountains that I decided contact was an absolute necessity.

My bike had been letting me down. I just didn't have the suspension or the ground clearance to keep up with the Yamahas, Ducatis, or even the '69 Harley FLH and had pretty well accepted that I'd be in Vegas a few days later than the rest of the Club. Wrong bike, wrong roads. I was tired and pissed off and there were still many days of humiliation ahead. And then there was this corner. The kind I would usually slow down for—if I'd had brakes. Tree-lined to one side with a five-hundred-foot drop into the blue-green valley on the other, it caught me by surprise. At fifty miles an hour, which was a lethal cornering speed on the stretch, I knew that I didn't have time to do much other than keep going. A few pumps on the front brake and I surrendered. I was either going to make it or not. And, miraculously, as if my own state of acceptance had relaxed the elongated skeleton of the stretch, the bike took the corner like one of those cartoon cars that lengthens and bends with the curves in the road. With only one dodgy moment, as the fat rear tire skid in the dirt on the far shoulder of the road, we were there, home and rubber side down, on the far side of the mountain.

It was a minor miracle in two-wheeled travel, and a private moment.

Well, not quite, because just as I was reciting my Hail Marys and thanking the Lord for my deliverance, he popped out of a bush. Not Jesus, but John. Pipe in one hand, camera in the other. Capturing my shit-eating grin for posterity.

That night we were rooming side by side and lured by a sweet smell that reminded me of Acapulco, I banged on his door.

Welcomed with a smile and an invitation, "You want to do a bowl?"

I wasn't sure. I hadn't smoked anything since London, and that was limited to the occasional pipeful of hash before climbing into my sensory deprivation tank. Grass was hard to come by in England and, unlike hash, it had always made me a bit paranoid.

Still, now that I had knocked and the offer had been made, I felt obliged to be sociable.

"Sure," I answered.

We went inside, closed the door and lit the pipe. The first toke was fine. The grass was good and by the third inhalation I felt the old nerves crawling up my spine. Perhaps a bit of conversation would put things right. For instance, how had John met the rest of the Club and become part of the ride?

It turned out that he operated a motorcycle safety school and had taught the wife of one of the road racers down the hall how to ride her Harley. That had been his initial connection, getting him an invite on their first big coast-to-coast ride. He'd been a member ever since.

A motorcycle safety instructor. That made sense, sort of, I thought as I settled down inside the sweet smell and inhaled my way to that place where every word and gesture has multiple levels of meaning. Oh, yes, it had been a while since I'd smoked, and this stuff was strong and getting stronger. How the hell did he ride on it? A safety instructor? Was he stoned when he taught his courses? Was riding stoned part of the curriculum? At the height of my silent mental interrogation he presented me with his business card.

I stared at it.

"I thought you said you ran a riding school?"

"I do that on the side," he answered.

I looked at the card again. It seemed very official and said something about the department of correction. I looked more closely.

Shit, I was sitting there, stoned out of my gourd with a cop.

It took several more hits from the bowl and another half hour of conversation to reach the conclusion that I was safe, at least from John.

After that, the road trip took on a much more relaxed perspective. The stretch collapsed, after decimating what was left of its shock absorbers during a bumpy mile of road construction, and I was assigned one of the loaner bikes, which was stored behind the wine racks in the back of the chase truck.

Unfortunately, during one of my morning polishing binges, I dragged the cloth against the alternator cable, disconnected it, and miles later, fried the battery.

I was stuck somewhere west of West Plains, Missouri. The rest of the boys were already across the border and screaming through Kansas, and I was sitting on a bench in front of a repair shop sipping a beer and contemplating a Greyhound ticket back to New York. I felt deserted.

Then I heard the rumble of a Harley and looked up to see John, riding back along the highway, searching. He spotted me and pulled in.

I won't forget the next eight hours.

The bike broke down three more times, the battery was gone and the alternator ruined. We pushed it through the heat, paid a few local cowboys to give us a jump start, eventually getting it rolling, only to take the wrong turn on the wrong road, ending up in a ditch. John swerved in time to avoid the drop but I went flying by, catching my right foot on the roll bar of his bike.

I knew my foot was a write-off the moment I heard the sharp snapping sound and felt the blinding pain. By the time I got the bike under control and stopped in the gravel it was already swelling and pressing hard against the inside of my boot.

A hundred and eighty miles from Wichita, our scheduled stop for the night, in the middle of nowhere, unable to walk. With darkness falling and no electrical system on my bike, which meant no lights, it was one of the most God forsaken feelings I've ever known.

And there was John, like an anchor, calm and cool, saying, "Hey, this'll be easy. I'll get close behind you so we've got taillights and you can use the beam from my headlamp. We'll take it real slow. No problem, we'll get there."

With my foot exploding inside my boot, we motored along at thirty or forty miles an hour, beneath a sliver of moon, through the darkness and the dust and sage, overtaken by hurtling trucks and drunked-up drivers in pickups. There were a few times when I considered calling it off, pulling over to the side of the road, getting off the bike and curling up in the brush to wait for morning. It was during those times that John, as if tuned in by some telepathy, would pull up beside me.

"Not much further now, keep it up, you're doing good," he'd say.

When my bike finally gave up completely, about thirty miles from Wichita, he lifted me off the saddle, flagged down a car and got me a ride to the hospital.

I learned to trust John that night. When all my hype and macho facade had given way and it got down to basics, he didn't let me down. That night we became friends.

After the trip ended and each of us returned to our working lives—in fact he was not a cop, but a corrections officer, an educator for delinquent boys—whenever I was in the United States and out on Long Island I'd try to meet up with him, sometimes taking my bike across the Sound for a ride on his side of the water. Helmets off, we'd ride the Connecticut roads, winding our way along the shore. Like me, he had a fascination with the outlaw biker culture and we often cruised by the Hell's Angels clubhouse on our way for a drink at their local bar. He seemed as at home in the company of outlaws as he was with the high rollers of the Bridge Club. He never ruffled.

Two years later, in the middle of a divorce, hurting inside, and wobbling, I rode my bike to John's. "Don't worry, I know what you need," he said, then laced me up with a jug full of margaritas, sat me down in a chair while he listened to me rant, and ended the evening with a CD of John Lee Hooker singing the blues.

In the time that I knew him, which covered a period—during his own divorce—when he lived in the unfinished basement of his mother's home, sleeping on a cot with his bike a few feet away in the garage—he was never judgmental. That was perhaps the greatest lesson of John. He seemed always to accept his circumstances and who he was, therefore accepting others in the same way. Maybe it was his job that taught him this. He often told me that the delinquent boys he had worked with could have been any of us, given the conditions and the environment. Some had stolen, some had murdered. "Mostly crimes of passion," he'd say.

There were no assholes in John's life, no crazies, no dullards. He didn't categorize or perceive people in that way. People were simply people.

I never saw him display anger.

Three weeks before he died we had another jug of margaritas. "I'm not sleeping too well," was his only complaint during a day spent with his girlfriend and two of his four daughters, holding my new son, and laughing a lot. It was the day he introduced me to the music of sixteen-year-old guitar genius Jonny Lang.

The last time we spoke, after the cancer had ravaged his body and the chemotherapy had robbed him of his long hair and dulled his eyes, his voice on the phone was not much more than a gurgle, the gasps of someone fighting for their last breaths. His words came in quick struggling spurts. Mostly he said my name, over and over again, as if it would keep us on the same side of some great divide. The last thing I spoke of was riding a motorcycle, and about how sometimes, you just have to let go and trust the bike to flow with the highway, into the wind and the sun. I believe John knew what I was talking about.

"Let everything go, relax, go for the ride," I said, almost pleading with him.

Two nights later he did, at home, with his Harley in the garage below his bedroom. He was forty-three years old.

And now, out here on the highway, the veil between life and death has lifted and, for a moment, we're riding together again.

I can sense him, and his presence makes me feel more whole, stronger, better for having learned from him and better for having experienced a bit of life with him.

"Let go," he says. "Just ride."

WHAT IS THE
COLOR OF WIND (Zen koan)

THE SILVER BIKE IS VERY SIMPLE. Everything about it is minimal, from the rigid steel frame—almost like a bicycle frame—to the short, drag style handlebars and single saddle, to the chopped fenders and ceramic coated exhaust pipes that connect to the 107 cubic inch engine.

I wanted it that way, and it occurs to me, as I roll along this ribbon of gray that will eventually take me to it, that I have been trying to find my way to the silver bike for many years, but it was in Sturgis, two years ago, that the underlying need took visual form.

It was my first morning in town and I was standing by myself in the exhibition lot off Lazalle Street, searching for a familiar face.

It is a big lot, behind the town's civic center, and during bike week it hosts many of the major motorcycle and custom designer displays. Big Dog rents space in the lot, as does American Iron Horse and Performance Machine. Every two-wheeled creation imaginable is either parked on the red carpets beneath the canopied marquees or is rumbling slowly by, gathering stares, on Lazalle Street Frames that have been stretched, molded, and chromed, tanks that have been reshaped and adorned in intricate detail by some of the best graphic artists in the world, protected by six coats of hard clear lacquer, all languish beneath a Midwestern sun that makes them explode in starbursts of multicolored glory.

Then there are the people.

Many are as customized as the bikes. This is a land where steroids and silicone have created a super race. Men in cutoff denim, their club colors stitched to their backs bearing names like Sons of Silence M.C., Vietnam Vets M.C., Sons of God M.C. From outlaws to ex-soldiers to evangelists, with arms like girders, etched in enough tattooed graphics to rival the aluminum and steel gas tanks of the show bikes. Women with celebrity chests, clad in butt-baring riding chaps, stroll the grounds, ogling the megapowered steel horses. Machines capable of transporting all this muscle and flesh to the neverending parade that transverses Main Street, a block away.

No stranger to boxing gyms, martial arts training halls, and weight rooms, and a competitor, in one way or another, most of my life, I was awed by the display. It was as if a comic book of fantasy machines, super heroes and villains had opened and its contents flowed to life. I had been dropped into the center of an arcade game.

Symbols were everywhere. Strength and power, speed and sexuality. Everything that man could project and manufacture. Beyond the smell of exhaust fumes and gasoline, the air held a wildness, an energy, and a roar.

Had it not been for the feeling of being somewhat overwhelmed I would not have paid any particular attention to the bike sitting in the far corner of the lot, behind a custom display. For me, it was a visual refuge. Rough and raw to look at, an engine bolted onto a basic rigid frame, with a one piece tank, drag bars, no front fender, a chopped rear fender, and a chain driven, fat rear tire. It was not even painted, just the bluish-gray color of rolled steel. Yet, in the midst of the paint, chrome and testosterone, it appeared grounded and pure.

Pointing at the bike, I asked the bearded man, busy working on another flashier machine in the back of the trailer, who owned it.

"Belongs to us. We haven't really started work on it," he answered, shrugging me off.

I wanted to tell him not to touch it, that it was perfect, that it had what none of the other bikes had, but I really didn't know what that was, not exactly, so I stood there for a few minutes, fixed on the steel skeleton.

A few minutes later, with Sheldon Coleman, owner of Big Dog Motorcycles, in tow, I was back.

"That's what I want," I said.

He studied the bike, but didn't answer.

"Bare to the bones," I continued.

I'm not certain he knew exactly what I was rambling on about. I didn't. All that I knew was that after fifteen years of buying them, stripping them down, and rebuilding them, I was still searching for something, and that this revelation had as much to do with myself as it did with the motorcycle.

The Taconic rolls and banks gently, with the slate-gray Hudson River snaking parallel to the highway. The Catskill Mountains are visible behind it; they seem to be levitating in the hot, humid air.

I'm doing sixty-five, which is fast enough to feel the surge of the bike, and slow enough to be enveloped in the smells of the forest which travel on the wind.

The difference between motoring around town, stopping every four or five miles, and riding the highway is the difference between the harbor and the deep blue sea.

Here, there are horizons, and the sense of liberation that the wide open space inspires. Nothing is familiar, not the landscape or the sky, but I feel at home. My mind is free.

I go twenty more miles before I realize that I haven't been thinking, at least not in the way I usually think, with the structured order that creates everyday reality. This is more a stream of consciousness, images from my past, the faces of people, lyrics to half-forgotten songs, people that I haven't seen or thought about in years. A college girl-friend. Where is she now? Alive or dead? Of all the people that I know or have known, who is alive? I am. Right now. I'm tingling with life. It's traveling like a current of elec-tricity, rushing up from the road, through the bike and into my body, coaxing my mind to euphoria.

The wind has color. It's silver with expectation.

I see a road sign. It reads, SARATOGA SPRINGS.

The wind changes, the color is blue.

AMSTERDAM

I AM SITTING IN THE GRASS, HALFWAY UP A HILL. The bike is sitting in the parking lot below me. It appears small, even tiny, against the backdrop of the river, the valleys, and the mountains. There is not a house or building in sight and the river now looks brown, long and thin, winding its way through the green.

Checking my watch I see that it is five o'clock.

I saw the road sign for Saratoga Springs about five minutes ago. That is the reason I pulled off, but something inside me has stalled.

Saratoga Springs is where four members of my family are buried: my grandmother, my grandfather, my uncle Richard, and my father.

I never knew my uncle, but I am at peace with my grandmother and grandfather.

I keep a secret regarding my father. It's something I am ashamed of, something I am not willing or able to face right now. It would not be an easy trip to his graveside. Besides, I had no idea that Saratoga Springs would be part of my trip. No idea that I was even close to it, not till the highway sign. It seems like a stroke of fate, and I feel the past pulling me back from the present.

I don't have the time to go there, I tell myself, getting up from the grass and walking back to the bike. I know I'm lying. This is not about time, it's about guilt.

Riding past the Saratoga Springs exit and continuing west along Route 90, the next few miles seem plagued with an internal gravity. Negative thought creates a negative reality. My trapezius muscles—the ones determined to hold my neck to my shoulders, while my helmeted head bobs in the wind like a balloon on a string—suddenly feel rigid and burning with sharp tingling pains.

I recall the last time I saw my dad. If I had passed him on the street I wouldn't have recognized him.

Then I think of grandpa. Old Richard G., with his flyaway toupee and British Bat.

He was ninety-four years old when we were last together, and his hairpiece had taken on a permanent tilt, the part drifting further and further toward his left ear while the right side had lifted, leaving a conspicuous gap between his shiny pink scalp and the meshed net beneath.

His final act, following an exhausting and fruitless session of waiting in line at the emergency ward of the local hospital while his chest pains increased, was to walk out of the place in disgust and drive himself home, possibly in reverse since in his last years he had become convinced that driving in reverse saved on gas mileage. There, he crawled into his bed, went to sleep, had a massive coronary and died.

Thoughts of him, looking into my eyes while adjusting the angle of his red plaid bow tie to match the thirty degree list of his hair and declaring, in his Londoner's English, "Certain people around this town think I'm eccentric, but what the hell do they know . . . ? Every day

I look at myself in the mirror and ask, 'Just who the hell do you think you are?' " Then, eyeing me through the thick lenses of his glasses, which were perched dead center on his large aquiline nose, he demanded, "I want you to do that, it's good exercise. Keeps you on the level."

Just who the hell do you think you are?

I'm still pondering the question when I notice a dark bank of clouds rolling in from the west.

It's followed by a light sprinkle of rain, enough to make the highway slick, and I give in to the fact that I am probably not going to make Buffalo by nightfall.

The rain gets harder. Still, it's not bad, just little needle pricks against my cheeks, and the bike seems perfectly stable on the corners, the traction is fine and the moisture is mildly refreshing after a day in the bake oven.

Another few minutes pass, with my attention riveted on the operation of the motorcycle. The temperature has dropped and I'm shivering.

Next exit, I promise myself.

I consider pulling over to the shoulder of the road in order to put on my leather jacket, just as I spot a sign for Amsterdam, New York.

Amsterdam. This trip truly seems to be some sort of family reunion. My grandmother was born in Amsterdam, in 1882. Her name was Adeline Belle Salisbury and in her eyes, I was an angel. Even when drunk, fighting, disorderly, or tossed out of school, I still could do no wrong.

I've never been to Amsterdam, but it seems a natural place to stop.

I ride into town by way of a bridge that crosses a railroad track and leads to a narrow two-lane road that climbs a hillside. The houses and buildings on either side are made of wood, most are in mild disrepair and look as if they date back to grandma's era, the early nineteen hundreds.

It's strange riding alone into Amsterdam, a small town, where my appearance is worthy of careful scrutiny. Even in the light rain, there are clusters of young men outside the local mini-market and my passing causes heads to turn and eyes to linger.

I wonder what their fantasy of me is. Do they sense that I am temporarily detached from my normal existence? Feeling singular and impermanent, a ghost, passing like a shadow across their eyes. My sense of them is confinement. I imagine myself living in one of the small houses that I ride by, working in one of the gas stations and shopping at the 7-11, marrying a local girl and waking up every morning to the sound of the train whistle as the express passes through en route to bigger cities and bigger lives. It has always been a fear of mine to be marooned in a place far from the ocean and far from a metropolis, connected only by television images and magazines. Then, maybe it's not that way at all. Maybe it's safe and secure, without the competition, without the baseball hats.

One of the beauties of motorcycle travel is that I can stop and find out. I can pull in, rent a room, and enter, for a brief spell, the spirit of the place.

The Best Western occupies a corner lot close to the train tracks and within a couple miles of 90 West, my escape route out of here, to Sturgis. The parking lot and entrance seem well lit and there is a wide paved area in front of the sliding glass doors. If I park the bike on the pavement it will put it in clear view of whoever is working the night shift at the reception desk. I rumble into the lot and mount the curb, then slowly ride the twenty feet to the entrance to the lobby. Looking through the plate glass I can see a red-haired woman behind the desk. She's studying me with an expression of mild concern mixed with curiosity, as if I might be intending to continue to ride, straight through the doors and into the lobby.

I pull as close to the building as I can, assuring a pas-
sageway for other guests, shut off the engine, and climb
off the bike. After nine hours in the saddle, I feel a bit
awkward on my feet. It's as if my body has begun to mutate to a permanent riding position. My shoulders are
hunched and stiff, my legs seem more bowed than usual
and my injured knee feels bloated and sore inside the
brace.

My hands tremble slightly as I shut off the petcock then
remove the lock from its storage position on the frame and
attach it to secure the rear wheel before checking the
tightness of various nuts and bolts as I make my way
around the motorcycle. I unbuckle the straps of the saddlebags and lift out the plastic garbage bags which contain
my personal belongings. One of them rips, giving way as
a bundle of socks, several T-shirts, and my shaving kit spill
to the ground. Bending down to gather them up, I realize
that I am both physically and mentally exhausted. Every
task seems suddenly monumental. Including the limping
walk to the reception desk, arms laden with helmet, twin
garbage bags, a few pairs of socks and a leather jacket.

"Are you working all night?" I ask the redhead.

She looks taken aback, as if she has just been proposi-
tioned by Bigfoot.

"Will you be able to keep an eye on my motorcycle," I
add by way of explanation.

She discreetly surveys my motley appearance while running my card through her computer. Answering "yes," as
the card clicks "approved," then assures me that the bike
will be safe and upon request, supplies me with a handful
of fresh plastic garbage bags for my wardrobe. I receive
them with thanks, although having become a bit of a connoisseur regarding the texture of bin liners, note that they

are thinner than the ones I am currently carrying as luggage and wonder how they will hold up to my current supply of underwear.

The room is on the third floor, overlooking the highway, and that's where the ritual begins. Everything is unpacked, laid out, and carefully examined, as if the contents of the plastic bags may have altered in appearance or function during the past few hundred miles. The truth is, the contents of the bags represent my state of mind at the beginning of the journey. The single, pressed denim shirt, brought along for purposes of formal dress, is rumpled and looks particularly ludicrous. At this moment I can hardly envision a situation in which a laundered and pressed shirt will be required dress. Then there are the espadrilles, lightweight white canvas slip-ons with rope soles. I had forgotten that I'd stuffed them down the side of the bag at the last minute and now can't think of why I did it. More suitable for a walk on the beach or a day in the tropics, I doubt if I'll be spending much time wearing them on the bike and certainly can't imagine shuffling through the dusty streets of Sturgis with espadrilles on my feet. They look like a leftover from Don Johnson's wardrobe in *Miami Vice*, out of place beside the rubbery-black synthetic cloth of my borrowed rainsuit.

Once I've got everything checked over, refolded, and reinserted into my new plastic suitcases, I disrobe and spend another fifteen minutes doing dekinking exercises, stretches and a few push-ups, followed by some straight-legged quadriceps lifts to assure the muscular support of my bogus knee. Following that it's a look in the mirror.

Just who the hell do you think you are?

The man staring back at me is not a stranger, but I realize that it has been a while since I've spent time alone with him. From Mexico to England, with a hundred hotel mirrors in between, I have studied this guy, witnessing his changes in the glass reflections. The physical process of age has been inevitable, but the eyes still hold a spark of humor and, I believe, the beginnings of acceptance.

Close on the heals of this inspection comes a careful cleaning of the lenses of my sunglasses, followed by several single-handed knife opening drills with the Timberline.

The rigors of martial arts training are followed by a hot bath and a furious battle to untie the knots in my hair. I quit halfway, with the look of a mad Rastaman, get dressed (boots, not rope soles) and amble down to the lobby.

My plans for a night exploring town are squelched by heavy rain and deep fatigue, so I settle into a red leatherette cubicle in the hotel's restaurant, sip a syrupy premixed margarita and pick at a bizarre concoction of lettuce leaves, bread sticks and peanut butter sauce that was advertised as a Thai chicken salad, making note never to order Thai food outside of a Thai restaurant again, while watching a muted baseball game on a wall-mounted television screen. Somewhere at the height of my culinary revelry I overhear a male voice from a booth close by.

"Did you see that thing outside?"

For some reason my ears perk up.

"Yeah, I did," another male voice answers.

"All alone."

My T-shirt squeaks as my back straightens against the vinyl.

"What do you reckon something like that's worth?"

I believe I detect a bit of a southern drawl in the voice whose owner is obviously—to me—talking about the Big Dog. I crane my neck to find them.

"Twenty grand, maybe more."

They are hunched low in their plastic foxhole.

"Probably a lot more."

I consider announcing myself as the owner of the bike and short-circuiting their plans to steal it but I can no longer hear them speaking so I ask for my bill and saunter by their table on my way to the door.

They don't look like bike thieves. They look like a couple of college kids, button-down collars and short hair and my intended proclamation seems a bit out of place. Besides I never actually heard them mention a motorcycle. Anyway, by the time one of them looks up and spots me I nod and keep moving, out the door of the restaurant and into the reception hall.

Yeah, but what if they are planning to take the bike? I ponder. I check the motorcycle through the window, it's my lifeline, my way in, my way out of here. It looks slightly different in color than it did when I parked it. The flames seem to have changed from purple to a neon blue, almost translucent which I put down to the overhead outdoor lights, conspiring with the mind-altering effects of the plastic margarita.

I hover a while, then go back to the desk. My bin liner connection has that look in her eyes that says, *Oh no, here he comes again.*

"You sure the bike's safe?" I ask.

"I'm here all night," she reassures me. I walk the beige carpeted corridors to the elevator and take the elevator back up to my room. Clothes off, I lie down on the bed.

Only three hundred miles and ten hours from when and where I started this morning, but I feel a long way from anything familiar. Things that seemed important—like having no place to live—are not important now. Nothing feels quite as important as it did yesterday. Except the bike.

Clothes back on. Espadrilles, not boots, I creep out of

the room and take the elevator down to the potential crime scene. And find it exactly as I left it, except the bike looks slightly more purple and the lady behind the desk looks down at her guest registry when she sees me approaching. A bit embarrassed I walk out and pretend to check my saddlebags while investigating to make certain that the chain is still secure. Everything is fine, but just be sure, on my way back to the elevator, I sneak a look into the dining room. The button-down collars have gone. So have I, mentally.

Back in my chamber, the view from the window, above the rooftops, is dark with night and rain. The ground and sky have merged. I consider turning on the television for an update on the weather but it doesn't matter. I'm going. Rain or shine, fast or slow, I'm going.

Espadrilles off—knew I'd need them—clothes off. Lights off. Into bed. There is peace inside the darkness, and the wind, rain, and drone of the highway seem distant.

The late Janis Joplin, a rock icon of the '60s, once said, "Did you ever consider that a lifetime is just one long day."

Eyes shut. This one's over.

DAY TWO

NO TIME TO WALLOW IN THE MIRE.

—THE DOORS

PLASTIC MAN

AT FIRST I THINK IT'S AN EARTHQUAKE. I was in one once in LA, staying in a fourth floor hotel room, and it felt something like this, as if the bed was on rollers. But I'm not moving, not exactly, it's more of a rumble beneath me, like a vibrating mattress.

I reach out for my wife and find an empty space beside me and a cold pillow above. Then a train whistle blows, big and hollow, reconnecting the pieces of my mind that I seem to have left in another place. I look to my left and see the digits of a bedside clock, hovering in the darkness, reading 4:30 A.M.

It would help if I knew where I was.

Sliding out of bed I walk to the window, pull back the heavy curtains and look out in time to see the tail-end of a freight train disappear, heading east along the tracks. The lonely whistle blows again, this time from farther away, and the floor of my room stops vibrating.

Amsterdam, I remember, home of the synthetic margarita.

The sky is covered by a lid of dark clouds and a light

fog has rolled in. The highway beneath the amber yellow glow of the overhead lights looks like an ice rink and the only things moving are trucks, one after another in a long steady procession in both directions.

I look around my room. In the dim light I see my jeans, my boots, my knee brace, my plastic luggage, my knife, and my breakfast, an oatmeal Power Bar, sitting on the coffee table beside a bottle of Saratoga Springs water.

Using well practiced fighting skills I flick open the Timberline and slice through the wrapper of the bar. My first bite into its sticky, honey-coated surface coincides with the sharp crack of thunder as the sky opens and the rain begins to fall in fat gray drops.

It's 4:45. There is absolutely no rush to get on the road before the flood subsides. It's not even sunrise. *Sit back, relax.* I tell myself. Think about the two thousand and some miles of highway between here and Sturgis. What if it rains all the way? Relax. Now there's the problem. I've lost the knack. My life is on a deadline, most of it self-imposed. Relax. It must be the best kept secret in modern living. Everyone I know lives on "call waiting."

This is my time off the hook, the solo cross-country ride I have fantasized about since I first bought a Harley-Davidson Sportster from Fred Warr's showroom in London, England in 1986. Then I'd sit in my third story office and stare out the window at bleak winter skies and a darkness that fell like a curtain at three-thirty in the afternoon while my bike sat in the garage of the house, a polished mirror of my discontent. With a marriage that was running on deadlines, culminating with my ex-wife's assistant suggesting I book lunch at least two weeks in advance to assure an opening in her (my ex-wife's) schedule. Thumbing through *Easyriders* magazine like an adolescent with his first copy of *Playboy*, devouring the pictures of the big bikes and the big American roads while day-dreaming of doing what I'm doing right now. Well, not exactly, it was always sunny in the pictures. This is more like an English morning on the Devon moors.

The last of the Power Bar clings to my rear molars as I hobble—must be the moisture in the air affecting my knee—to the window and investigate again. The rain has eased to a moderate downpour and there is no sign of a break in the clouds.

It's 5 A.M. and the possibility of holing up in the hotel room, consuming my supply of Power Bars and watching cable TV for the next few hours crosses my mind. At times like these it's comforting to feel that I have options. A few margaritas at lunch, maybe another Thai rubber salad for dinner and I could spend the week exploring Amsterdam, then catching up on celebrity gossip from the *National Enquirer* or *Inside Edition* on the TV. But that's not why I'm here. I'm riding away from life as portrayed on the small screen, from a constant bombardment in which even the most catastrophic personal problems are given the veneer of Hollywood glamor, spreading the feeling that there's never enough, of anything.

This is my purge.

Knee brace on, a trip to the bathroom and a tussle with a toilet seat that has been constructed from what I believe is the same material used by the bartender and kitchen staff. It's plastic, light, and thin and will not stay up no matter how delicately I try to balance it, creating a minor hygiene problem, particularly since my support brace inhibits my bowl side mobility.

Then a dip into the bin liner to get my rainsuit.

Black and folded and I have never even tried the rainsuit on. Actually it's a loaner, like the bike, and comes from Nancy, a lady in Dallas, Texas. She and her mate, Big Jim, are biking friends.

"Cross-country? Alone? You need a rainsuit and a handgun," he informed me, silver hair streaming down his back like the mane of a rogue lion. There was a zealous glint in his hazel eyes.

"The suit's here and we can send you the Glock, a nice light subcompact, polymer frame (plastic) eight in the clip and one in the chamber. It'll fit in your pocket."

As he spoke I remembered a time, during the Club run from New York to Las Vegas that my late friend John and I were stranded by the side of the road in Oklahoma, the battery on the Heritage fried and not a soul in sight. Until thunder from the highway, a cloud of dust and an old Pontiac GTO roared into view, like something from a *Mad Max* film, screeching to a halt about ten feet from my disabled bike. The muscle car's driver was equally prehistoric, large, sinewy, with a body suit of ink, featuring a jagged blue line tattooed around his neck, with "Cut here" tastefully inscribed beneath the art.

"Your motor broke down?" He asked behind a hopeful sneer.

I lied. "No, we're just taking a rest."

It may have been because it was a hundred and two degrees in the shade, which was limited to the shadow of the broken bike, but I could tell by the way he circled the Heritage, like an appraiser before the auction, that he didn't believe me.

"This motorcycle here looks like it's worth some money," he commented.

I've learned from my years on various roads that in times of threat and intimidation it's best to stay monosyllabic.

"Yep."

"Me an' my buddies lift a lota' dead bikes off this road," he continued with the hint of challenge in his voice. "You sure this one ain't dead?"

Meanwhile John had walked back to his Electraglide and was calmly unhitching the straps on one of his saddlebags. I vaguely wondered what he was doing and why he was deserting me.

"I'm sure," I answered.

"Bad place to be stuck," he added, looking out at the flat prairie plains, brown from drought, then directly into my eyes. "You boys are a long way from home."

I heard a click, like metal smacking against metal as we both turned to see John snapping the clip into a black automatic. Until then I'd had no idea he was packing a handgun. He wasn't aiming or pointing it; it was simply there, resting in his palm, but the threat was implied.

"That car of yours fast?" I asked, turning the tables.

"Fast enough," our visitor answered, already making tracks for the GTO.

He peeled out, spraying us with dirt and gravel as I turned to see John lower the weapon, placing it back in his saddlebag.

A few minutes later I hitched a ride in a pickup truck, heading for a service station and a set of battery cables, leaving John to watch over the bikes.

When I returned, with a mechanic, John was seated on the shady side of the big Glide, his saddlebags closed and belted. The gun was nowhere in sight.

Neither of us ever mentioned the incident again, but it was a strange feeling to know that John was armed and obviously prepared to defend our property. It wasn't a show or a game and I doubt if he was practicing fast draws in his hotel room mirror at night.

Unlike my Texan friends, to whom carrying a firearm is

as natural as line dancing in a pair of Tony Lamas, I have
had little experience with anything more lethal than a Red
Ryder carbine, shooting BBs at a target in my basement,
and that was over forty years ago. Plus New York is rigid
about issuing concealed carry permits, so I declined the
Glock, although it did inspire a few *Dirty Harry* fantasies.

The rainsuit, however, was a different matter. I can no
longer count the number of times that I've been caught,
in T-shirt and jeans, sopping wet and cursing, while my
sodden gloved hands tremble on the controls of the motorcycle. I have at last, for the most part, learned that
biking requires a degree of preparedness. Problem is that
another part of me, yet untouched by this wisdom or any
other form of common sense, tends to be short-sighted. If
it's sunny and ninety degrees in Dallas, I believe that it
will be sunny and ninety degrees everywhere else in the
universe, forever. However, urged by Big Jim, I did borrow
the rainsuit, agreeing to return it to them in Sturgis, following my ride. Secretly thinking, because of the weather
while I was in Dallas, that I wouldn't really be using it. I
didn't bother to try it on.

Now as I unfold it for the first time, I notice that it
seems small, which would make sense considering Nancy
is probably a shade under five-foot-six and weighs no more
than a hundred and thirty pounds. Which accounts for
the slight tear in the rear end as I pull it up and over my
jeans while the elasticized bottoms settle at my midcalf
mark, giving the distinct appearance that I am anticipating
high tides. Next I pull on my cowboy boots, then just to
be optimistic, coat my face with SPF 40 sunscreen, particularly over the area of my forehead above my eyes and
my nose. It's the kind of thing I may forget in my revelry
if the weather breaks and the sun shines.

My final statement, Samurai to the last, is to throw yesterday's socks into the waste bin.

Out the door before sunrise, or since there isn't going to be any sunrise, out the door before six A.M., fully packed, rainsuit on, and all the high octane of my partially digested Power Bar coursing through my veins.

Where I confront the next great paranoia. Theft. Will the motorcycle still be where I left it? Whenever I am out of sight of the bike for more than a few minutes, eating in restaurants, sleeping in trailers, or tents, or hotels, I have the fear. No matter that it's locked and chained to a post or railing. I've seen bolt cutters able to go through even the high-tempered "unbreakable" steel in seconds.

And I'm not forgetting last night's Ivy League bandits.

The elevator clanks to a halt, the door opens and I step out into the muted glow of the carpeted corridor, clad in tight black polyester, a bin liner in each hand, fighting knife in boot, and a helmet hung like a teacup from my pinkie.

My eyes are trained like a Doberman's on the plate glass window, where the Big Dog sits, glimmering beneath a fine sheen of water, saddle dripping.

Ready to ride.

FACTOR FORTY

THANK GOD FOR THE GOGGLES. I waved them off as totally unnecessary when my wife offered them to me a day or two before she left for Greece. She's practical, the kind of person who balances the checkbook and questions my expenditures on such things as typhoon carburetors and eighty-spoke wheels. In her biking days, premotherhood, when she rode a customized black Sportster and we were traveling from London to the coast in Devon, a trip of about two hundred miles, and hit a patch of the inevitable English rain, I remember her breaking them out from her back-pack, pulling them on over her helmet to my cackles and cries of "nice look, four eyes!"

I refused the same goggles a few days ago, but she stuffed them in my garbage bags anyway, hidden secretly inside a pair of socks. Now they're saving my eyeballs from a battering, but not from the sunscreen, which is running with the rivulets of rain down from my forehead, slipping past the rim of the goggles and bathing them in an acid-wash.

The factor forty is blinding me, which is not good since I'm locked in between a flat bed carrying a cargo of lumber and a very pushy BMW, intent on passing both of us but unable to because we're on a single lane section of Route 90 and there is traffic coming in the opposite direction.

If I wipe beneath the goggles the stinging sensation turns into something that feels like grains of sand being massaged into my eyeballs, causing a flood of tears, so I squint and endure the torture, looking for a wide shoulder or anything that resembles a rest stop, intending to pull in and clean up. Before that happens, a miracle occurs. The rain stops. The change is abrupt, as if I have crossed the divide between hell and heaven, and within a few minutes I am warm, my face has dried, the stinging in my eyes has stopped and the highway has changed into a freshly surfaced two-laner, passing down through green valleys and up gentle hills. The bike is humming and I'm beginning to unwind for the first time since that lonely whistle blew at 4:30 A.M. Bound for the silver bike. Bound for simplicity, which, it occurs to me, is what I've been trying to find for the past several years, ever since my ex-wife's final war cry of "get on that bike and get out of here!"

"Here" was Ravenswood House, a large, vine-covered nineteenth century manor on the crest of Kingston Hill, about ten miles from the center of London. "Here" was five fireplaces, stone archways, an indoor swimming pool, a forty foot gymnasium, and a sensory deprivation tank that I lay in like a Fiberglas coffin, drifting in darkness on salt water heated to body temperature, listening to piped in Zen meditation music and wondering why I was going nuts. "Here" was a marriage that after eighteen years had hit the rocks. Our values had diverged. She had become a successful TV writer-producer and lived the hype, resplendent with star-studded show biz dinner parties and late nights spent glued to the rushes from her most recent television productions, while I countered with increasingly long hours in the garage, polishing the chromed tailpipes of my Harley. It was close to sex, but something was missing.

I finally made the decision to go, but true to her newly acquired celebrity status she needed that last shout, "Get on that bike and get out!"

I did.

On a gray morning in February, in the middle of a cold damp English winter, with the bare necessities—toothbrush, underclothes and a razor—crammed down the front of my leather jacket. I got out hanging on to my balls by a thread. Headed for a five room apartment overlooking Saville Row, home of the bowler hat and James Bond's tailors.

I may have subconsciously wanted simplicity but I was hardly ready for a stone fortress heated by a single coal burning fireplace, with a Japanese-style toilet dug straight into the floor. There were no beds, simply a thin futon on a tatami mat and bathing facilities centered around a deep wooden bathtub, imported directly from Kyoto.

Secure behind locked gates and guarded by porters wielding cricket bats, I owed my new residence to my great friend Terence Stamp, distinguished actor, '60s icon, and organic guru. He was, at the time of my demise, out of the country filming.

"My place is open. Use it for as long as you need to," were his prophetic words when I informed him by phone that I may soon be homeless.

The ride was lonelier than a full night in the flotation tank.

His place, or "set," as apartments are termed at Albany, was in one of the original gentleman's quarters in Europe (ladies were finally accepted in the mid-eighteen hundreds), a much sought after oasis in the heart of town. It may have been 1995 in Piccadilly Circus, but behind the red-brick façade of Albany's porters' lodge and up the tree-lined walk-way that led to G3, it was always 1776—although aside from Stamp, most sets had bowed to the modern wonder of central heating.

My arrival was met by two porters with cricket bats fol-lowed by a fire engine. Later I learned that a resident, awakened from a tea-time slumber by the bellowing of my exhaust pipes and the stink of the Harley's leaded fuel had thought a bomb had been set off by the IRA and dialed Emergency. Only the mention of Stamp's name saved me from possible head wounds and instant eviction.

While my soon to be ex-wife, now known in English theatrical circles as the Diva, informed mutual friends that I had suffered a psychotic breakdown and lost my mind before announcing on national television that she was per-forming voodoo rites on a doll made in my image, I win-tered at Albany. Lugging buckets of coal three flights up stone steps from the cellar, developing the muscles of my thighs by performing full squats above the sunken toilet bowl, sipping from liter bottles of saki while soaking in water up to my chin in the wooden bathtub and sleeping on the hard mat above the tatami floor, without the dis-traction of a television, a radio, and free from the theat-rical "darlings" of Ravenswood.

The Harley Springer, a black hole in my credit card and a symbol of my diminished masculinity, weathered outside beneath a tarpaulin. It was often wet, and being my sole means of conveyance, was finally used to ride. Polishing fell to an avocation.

As the winter got colder, the baths got hotter and longer.

It was during this period of saki-soaked introspection that I designed my first mail order motorcycle.

R.U.B.B.
(Rich Urban Bike Builder)

IT HAD TO BE POWERFUL, IT HAD TO HAVE SUSPENSION, and it had to have saddlebags. Practical would be a one word definition, as opposed to the roaring excess that was chained below, representing about fifty thousand dollars of trial, error, and maxed out credit cards. Not that I didn't love the Springer. I did. It was my work of art, it's just that every journey over the distance of five miles had begun to cost me, something was either vibrating loose or falling off. I think I was averaging about a hundred bucks a ride. On top of which I knew it would never pass emissions control standards in New York, which is where I planned to live when my divorce was finalized. Without turn signals and mirrors, it wouldn't even pass the state inspection. My plan was that the Springer would stay in England while I, mounted on my new highway cruiser, would soul-search my way across the landscapes of America. I had gone from Rich Urban Biker to Rich Urban Bike Builder, the long distance wrench.

The reality that I was far from rich didn't stop me.

I had a dream. I also had friends in the American motorcycle business. Plus, I had barter, in the form of a Harley Softail that I had been forced to leave in Wichita, Kansas after my failed attempt to ride it to Las Vegas. Lowered, modified, and with the frame stretched to seat a six-foot-seven-inch basketball player comfortably, at five-feet-nine, I had a problem riding it in any other way than in a straight line.

The bike had been trucked to Wichita, where Big Dog had rebuilt it from the engine to the paint. The frame, unfortunately, remained long and low, while I remained five-feet-nine.

Sheldon Coleman, leather jacket, blue jeans, and Gucci loafers, founded Big Dog Motorcycles in 1993. He was one of the first to see a gap in the American market for custom-built motorcycles, created by people like myself, who would start with a stock Harley-Davidson, then piece by piece replace everything but the frame. It generally doubled the cost of the original bike, but in my case, because of a personality disorder (I'm sure my ex-wife would confirm), I managed to quadruple the original price of both my bikes.

The philosophy of the new companies was simple: begin with a frame, not a stock motorcycle, then add all the best aftermarket components, performance parts and custom pieces that money can buy. Build the Rolls Royce of motorcycles. It was expensive, but at least you were starting from zero and not fifteen thousand below.

Coleman is a man with real money, enough to run Big Dog Motorcycles out of his pocket. He comes from a long line of highly successful business people, his grandfather having started The Coleman Company in 1901 (famous for camping equipment). He loves motorcycles, in fact it was Sheldon who organized the cross-country run to Vegas in which I distinguished myself in by wrecking two bikes and breaking my foot.

As comfortable standing in front of the Big Dog trailer during bike week talking single spark ignitions with hardened road warriors as he is in a dinner jacket sipping champagne at a Palm Springs social function, Sheldon Coleman is a man for all seasons, smart enough to surround himself with a team who love and understand the motorcycle and the motorcycle business, from builders and mechanics to the sales crew.

I knew, with Big Dog, that not only would I get my bike, but that the company would stand behind it, always a deciding factor when investing twenty grand. There are a number of undercapitalized companies, turning up at shows and rallies with impressive machines, used as examples of their work. Taking orders that they are unable to fill, resulting in lots of lost deposits, and probably a few all-expense paid holidays in the Bahamas.

My conversation with Sheldon went something like, "If I send you a drawing of what I want, can you build it?"

"Yes."

"How long will it take?"

"About ninety days."

"You know that bike of mine that you rebuilt, the Softail?"

"Sure, it's sitting in the showroom right now. It gets a lot of attention."

"Can you sell it?"

"Probably."

"How about an even trade for whatever it is that I send you?"

Hesitation, then, "Just what are you planning on sending me?"

"Something with saddlebags," I answered.

"We've got plenty of great saddlebags."

"Good, we'll build a bike around them."

Designing the new bike became a great diversion from the ugly side of divorce. I spent many late nights by the coal fire, scribbling on a legal pad, coming up with things that looked like a kid's first two-wheeler, plain and fat, with saddlebags.

Big Dog did their part by shipping me piles and piles of catalogues, advertising everything from frames to saddles, replacing *Easyriders* as my preferred bedtime reading.

By day I tried to write a novel. Afternoons would occasionally include a visit to my divorce lawyer, aptly named Raymond Tooth, and sometimes there would be a meeting with both lawyers—his and hers—and the Diva, who now sported a floral tattoo that covered a good portion of her back and, at five-foot-two in stilettos, and wearing dark glasses while puffing a thin cigar, looked to me like a miniature Mafia Don.

By night I was constructing my escape vehicle.

Based on a rubber mounted frame—to limit the vibration of the engine—and powered by an eighty-eight cubic inch S&S engine with Edelbrock heads, the bike began to resemble a souped-up Harley Heritage.

After a month, the Polaroids began to arrive, showing the motorcycle in its early phases of development, the chassis; the chassis and tank; chassis, tank and handlebars—also a letter identifying its fabricator, a man identified as Mohawk, seen only as a dark, shadowy presence in the background of the grainy snapshots.

When I asked Willy, Big Dog's baritone voice on the telephone, exactly who Mohawk was, his answer included a description of Mohawk's trademark hairstyle and something about Mosh (later discovered to be all male, staged in a pit, and involving an enormous amount of hard phys-

ical contact, equivalent to the Ultimate Fighting Competition performed to the demonic sounds of bands like Rage
Against the Machine). Willy assured me that I'd meet the
man himself because it was, in fact, Mohawk who would
truck the bike to Long Island.

Building long distance became the high point of my
winter season, although the Japanese bathtub provided its
own steamy brand of mirth. Whenever things on the personal front seemed intolerable there was reprieve in the
form of a new set of Polaroids from Wichita, or a new
catalogue—exhaust pipes figured heavily in my psycholog-
ical rehab program. Even though I had never met Willy or
Mohawk I considered them, right up there with Ray
Tooth, among my strongest allies. I was in Sing Sing and
they were digging the tunnel out. I saw myself, long hair
streaming behind me like a banner of freedom, riding
through the badlands of New Mexico, or scaling the
mountain summits of Colorado, at one with my highway
cruiser, on the road to . . .

ONE MILE AT A TIME

BUFFALO, WHICH IS STILL ABOUT TWO HUNDRED MILES AWAY.
A very disquieting thought when stuck in the sprinter's
position, bent forward, ass in the air, chest parallel to the
gas tank, arms bent as if at the midway point in a press-
up with head aimed out and over the center of the handlebars. Chin down, minimizing wind resistance, with
eyeballs rolled upward in their sockets, struggling for a
view of the road. This awkward stance has been imposed
upon me by gusting sidewinds and periods of fog so thick
that the beam from my headlight looks like it's being reflected off a mirror directly in front of the bike.

Needless to say, heaven has reverted to hell. Just as I
was getting into the gentle curves of the highway, the
scent of the air cleansed by morning's rain, and the lush
green beauty of countryside, everything changed. First the
wind picked up, then the road began to rise and fall, dip-
ping into valleys where the mist hangs like a gray curtain,
dividing daylight from darkness. This is pull-off-and-wait-
it-out kind of stuff, but because there is no visible place
to pull over and because these patches last only as long

as it takes me to ride up the other side of the hill, I keep on going, using my index finger as a wiper blade to demist my goggles.

I continue like this for an indeterminable period, measured only by a buildup in my bladder, increasing the already considerable pressure behind the tight waistband of Nancy's rainsuit.

Finally, just as I have reconciled myself to a life in purgatory, it's out of the darkness and into the light.

Past Syracuse, through the Montezuma Swamp, where I stop for roadside relief in the marshlands, then on to a straight flat patch of macadam that travels through the Finger Lakes region of New York—named because of the long, thin lakes that spread fingerlike from Auburn to Canandaigua.

To my right, I spy a road sign for Geneva, New York. Home to Hobart College, a small, not quite Ivy League men's school, where thirty-five years ago I studied the ways of alcohol. Coming from Pennsylvania, with a drinking age of twenty-one, to New York, where eighteen would legalize a stool at the local bar, I took full advantage of my education. The same ass—younger and less wrinkled— that is trailing me now was revealed in all its pink-cheeked glory to many a man and his date following a beer-stained evening at the Twin Oaks tavern. Mooning, the sport of dropping your pants to display rear cleavage, was very popular at Hobart and I was a champion. Usually, following an evening's athletics, I ended bent over a toilet bowl, examining my lunch and vowing never to drink again.

I lasted a year in Geneva—before I was tossed out.

Then it was down south to Atlanta, Georgia to enroll in Oglethorpe College and an enlistment in the Officers Training Program of the United States Marine Corps. My military service ended with the crashed Norton, resulting in the destruction of my left knee, which, in 1968, probably saved me from a one-way trip to Vietnam.

Motorcycles have always figured heavily in my karma, not only reflecting my state of mind but often influencing the direction of my life.

The mail-order custom arrived in Amagansett, New York, before I did. Tied down like a prize bull in the back of a Dodge pickup with the much anticipated Mohawk at the wheel.

It was unfortunate that at five o'clock in the morning, after driving straight through the night, he got confused and picked the only cottage on Treasure Island Drive that had a car parked in front of it. Being off-season at the beach, every other place, including the one I had rented was vacant. This particular cottage belonged to sixty-some-year-old Ruthie B., property agent and single lady. She was tentative enough about living, isolated, in the dunes during the winter months and the appearance at that hour of a muscular gentleman with his head shaved to the bone on both sides while the hair in the middle stood up like a privet hedge, banging on her door, sent her into shock. Only Mohawk's gentle manner and mention of my name saved Ruthie B. from complete trauma.

By the time I arrived from London—later that afternoon—weary from the divorce wars, Mohawk was a legend, at least in Amagansett Wines and Spirits, owned by a biking friend, who had been kind enough to give Mohawk's pickup a berth in the parking lot behind the shop.

The Highway Cruiser was rolled down the rear ramp and after instructions regarding the amount of choke to give the cold engine and warnings about the quick grab of the Performance Machine brakes, I took a maiden voyage up Highway 27 toward Montauk, at the tip of the island.

The bike reminded me of my dad's '55 Buick—it was fat, stable, and luxurious, like a black blimp, with flashing indicators, floorboards, and lots of saddle room. Also very responsive considering I was used to riding a bored-out ninety-six cubic inch rocket with a postage stamp–sized saddle, and I hardly felt the road, which in those days was rough between Amagansett and Montauk. I hadn't been on anything with suspension in so long I didn't exactly trust it. It was the feeling of absolute connection that I missed, when every joint in the macadam is a chiropractic adjustment to the spine and every pothole a rabbit punch to the kidneys. Somehow, in personal and biking life, punishment had begun to correlate with reality.

Obviously, I needed to level out and ride on springs.

Michael, owner of the wine shop, took a spin after I returned and gave the Cruiser his seal of approval, although nothing, including suspension, electric starter, even brakes, would ever replace his decrepit '69 Harley FLH, which had carried him twice across America. He is, after all, a connoisseur and in his considered opinion, bikes, like wine, become more distinct with age.

Mohawk was proud of his creation, he had put it together from the frame up, following my basic drawings and suggestions and adding his own touches in the performance department. He knew every nut and bolt on the motorcycle, but after a few minor adjustments, both he and his traveling companion, an exotic dancer from Wichita, had begun to wilt. They had both gone forty-eight hours without sleep and even the suggestion of a round of Mosh in the parking lot didn't stir him, so I volunteered my cottage, took the Cruiser and headed east to a friend's house for the night.

The next morning, when I went to check in on them,

the mantlepiece above the fireplace was decorated with an artful series of Polaroids featuring Mohawk's tiny dancer emerging topless from the Atlantic Ocean, which in early November must have been all of fifty degrees.

The sun was shining but there was frost on the ground.

The man himself, bare chested and tattooed, towel in hand, put it simply.

"Water was a little cold but we had a great time on the beach."

It was the first that either of them had ever seen the ocean.

For me, Mohawk and his girlfriend were a breath of air, fresh and unaffected, a dose of the plain, simple honesty that I had lost in the ambitious, cutthroat circles of my former life.

It is an honesty that I have often found with bikes and the people who ride them.

It is that kind of honesty that I am looking for now, in myself, a rekindling of that part of me that has remained pure and untainted by pressures, personal fears, and uncertainties.

I'm fifty-four years old. Every time I turn around some doctor wants to take a poke at my prostate or my colon, or test my heart and blood. I'm going to die, it's just that I've never been made so aware of that fact as in the past few years. I have a three-year-old son. I have a pregnant wife. We have no place to live. We want to build a house. I earn a living writing books. I've never been on a best-seller list. What if I get sick? What if I don't get to see my children grow up?

What if?

Tensions that manifest in the mind end up in the body

and the bike is a catharsis, a release, an exercise machine capable of freeing each part of my self from this toxic buildup. It is medicine on wheels.

If the fog, the wind, and the rain have a single lesson to teach it is to accept the situation, to ride as well as I am able, to know my limits, to trust my judgment, to become self-reliant.

More than one person warned me about undertaking a long journey alone, forecasting crashes, breakdowns, and bandits, yet not one of them had ever done it. It was mostly conjecture, rising out of armchair fantasies and paranoias, compounded by a continual bombardment from the media, turning every word of bad news, from school shootings to blizzards, into soap opera.

"Take one mile at a time," was the best advice I received.

BUFFALO

THE ADIVCE, "TAKE ONE MILE AT A TIME," came from Jim
Bush in Buffalo, a city that as I ride through looks slightly
tarnished, even beneath the summer sun, like it has seen
better days and better times.

I pull off Route 90 at the first exit past the art museum
and into a service station, filling the tank of the bike before
calling Jim from my cell phone.

Fifteen minutes later his silver, tint-window van rolls
into the lot. He hops out, his head freshly shaved and
tanned, glistening in the afternoon heat.

"Nice ride?" he asks.

At that moment the rain, the fog, the wet roads, and
the trucks seem distant, like maybe they never happened.
All I can feel is the sun on my neck and my clearest memory is the surge of the bike on the open road. Like a sailor
on shore leave, I've still got the motion of the ship inside
me.

"Great," I answer, meaning it.

Jim has the usual cigar in his mouth, and his muscular
arms dangle from short sleeves. Not long ago the Marine

Corps set up a recruitment station at the Erie County Fair offering an official U.S.M.C. T-shirt to any man able to perform twenty-five chin-ups from a dead hang on a horizontal bar.

Jim hauled himself up nineteen times, which was about nine more than any of the other young bucks managed on that particular afternoon. Still, no T-shirt, even though he was three decades older than most of his competition.

He's a professional photographer and has been taking pictures for thirty years. In that time has produced photo spreads of at least a hundred custom motorcycles. My silver bike was one of them.

My original idea of a simple machine did not include paint. I wanted a motorcycle that was bare metal. I had seen a similar thing done by John Warr in London, to a Harley Wide Glide. He had removed the paint from the tank and fenders of the stock bike and using ultralight wire wool, hand-rubbed it till the metal looked like polished silver, then protected it with half a dozen coats of clear lacquer. In the bright sunlight—rare in London, which made it even more magical—it was possible to see every hair-thin groove that the soft wool had etched into the metal.

When putting the components of my new bike together, one of the first things I acquired, after the rigid frame, was a one-piece stretched aluminum gas tank, manufactured by Battistinis in Bournemouth, England.

Rikki and Dean Battistini were among the first to create custom bikes on that side of the Atlantic and I had known both from the beginning of their business, having worked with them on the Springer and the Softail. Many of the design concepts on those bikes—which were among the first English shop customs—were due to Dean and Rikki.

Sadly, Dean, mild-mannered and very patient when it
came to getting things right, died in France, the result of
a motorcycling accident that, ironically, took place during
the making of a promotional film for their company. Rikki
continued the business and I wanted a reminder of them
on the American bike, so I ordered the tank.

The first time I laid eyes on the Silver Bike was in Daytona, Florida. It was during bike week, my first time in
town, and I was driving down the main drag looking for
the Big Dog trailer. The place was bumper to bumper, bike
to bike, with bands playing and bikini babes strutting a
full array of silicone enhancements. My mind was di-
verted. I was lost. I was ogling. I was trying not to run
over any of the patch wearing, bike riding outlaws with
my rental car, an electric blue Neon, while keeping one
eye peeled for my bike.

And there it was, muscular and low to the ground,
parked on its stand in front of the red trailer. I had drawn
pictures of it, sent faxes, seen Polaroids, and finally it was
staring me in the face, like a mail-order bride. I would
have recognized it anywhere, but in Daytona, in a sea of
fancy paint and dazzling chrome, the plain Silver Bike was
an anchor to my senses.

It was the first time I'd met the builder, Frank Aliano,
face to face, although I'd come to know his voice on the
phone as well as my own brother's. It was sort of like
shaking hands with the obstetrician after he delivers you
a perfect baby.

The bike wasn't quite finished and nobody was certain
if the brushed metal would hold up to the salt air of Eastern Long Island, but I took it home anyway.

I rode it through the summer, as drop by drop the moisture slipped beneath the clear coat and began to rust
everything but the aluminum tank. It was still in its early

phases, minor discoloration here and there, almost imperceptible, but it was spreading.

I called John Warr in London and he said they'd had the same problem with the Wide Glide and had, finally, ended up painting it.

Then I called Big Dog and decided on a powder coat of silver.

There were a few other changes to make, both aesthetically and technically, so the Silver Bike was going back to Wichita, but not before Jim Bush got to town.

He'd been given the assignment of photographing the bike as a feature for *Easyriders* magazine—sort of like an Academy Award in American Biking—and it was to be adorned with the latest winner of the Fox Hunt competition.

The Fox Hunt is an amateur tits-and-ass contest, in which readers of the magazine or their enthusiastic boyfriends submit Polaroids of the hopeful Fox in all her barebreasted splendor. God help those submissions of anything below Pamela Anderson proportions because the readers of *Easyriders* like their mammaries large. Each entry also includes a line or two, supposedly written by the contestant, as to how or why she got into motorcycles. Claims that the the first ride was so awesome that "I left a wet patch on the saddle" are customary. Based on the merit of the orbs, the face above them, and the passion of the accompanying poetry, the readers vote on who the winner will be.

Jim hired the studio of the local television station for the shoot and Mandy arrived, from the Bronx, by limo.

Her boyfriend, who had paid for her pectoral enhancements, had developed cold feet after she'd won, expressing concern about the possibility of his girl being molested by a gang of wild bikers, but Jim put things right by turning the photo session into a family affair. In other words he had invited me, my wife, and my then two-year-old son, Jack, to Mandy's unveiling.

The silver bike was heroically positioned against a moody gray backdrop, strobe lights were flashing, while Jim was adjusting the lens on his five thousand dollar Hasselblad camera. Mandy was behind the thin door of her improvised dressing room, changing from her street clothes into the first in her selection of costumes. The TV boys, who had rigged the dressing room up with a folding chair, card table, small mirror, and bottle of Perrier, were pressed flat-nosed against the window of the studio door, peering in, desperate for a glimpse of the goods.

Finally she emerged, wearing a luminescent pink string bikini and very high heels. Walking straight to the bike, straddling the saddle, gripping the tank gently, bending provocatively over the handlebars, legs straight, back arched, rear end held proud and high, front end in full extension. Hitting her first pose while Jim got off a fast volley of shots. *Snap. Snap. Snap.* Then another caress of the chrome, pout of the lips, tilt of the hips, and she was riding sidesaddle—the girl was a pro and the bike loved her. So did the guys behind the window of the studio door as evidenced by the steamy glass and their muffled shouts of encouragement which forced a time-out as Jim chased them away. After that things went into high gear, with Jim matching Mandy pose for pose, kneeling, squatting, balanced on his toes, switching backdrops, changing cameras, all the while encouraging her as she got down to the basics of biker photography, at last whipping off the top of her bikini to reveal several thousand dollars worth of enlargement.

My wife stood respectfully while I wondered if Mandy's assets would somehow compromise the Zen beauty of my rolling art.

It was only my son Jack who reacted in true biker fashion.

Not long off the tit—albeit his mother's—he moved quickly and aggressively, elbowing Jim out of the way in a mad dash to the mams. Reaching up, as Mandy, taken by surprise, teetered on her spikes. Jack latched on with both hands, and once contact was established he wasn't letting go. For a moment it was in doubt as to how far Mandy's professional courtesy would extend.

Then, in a show of motherly instinct, kindness, and good humor, she bent down and lifted Jack up in her arms, allowing him full access to what many behind the window had only dreamed of.

Turning to us, she observed, "He's a tit man, isn't he?"

I follow Jim through the streets of Buffalo and into the west side of town, to a 15,000 square foot red brick building that, a hundred years ago, was a horse stable and blacksmith shop. Now it is Jim's home and the center of his photographic business, including a loft that he occupies with his family, offices for his business, a studio and developing rooms.

The first thing I see as I ride the bike up the ramp and into the far end of the huge studio space is a Sapphire Sunglow '92 Softail Custom. The Harley sits low to the ground, clean and shining like a blue-green gem.

After I shut off my engine and ease the morning's kinks from my legs and shoulders we take a closer look at the bike, which like the English Springer has been fitted with a set of Branch heads, the place at the top of the engine where the gas meets the oxygen, meaning that the stock inlet and outlet valves have been ported—smoothed out, by adding bits of metal in certain places, removing them in others—and polished till they shine, making the combustion more efficient and the bike go faster. There is an art to getting the correct balance with the metal, not to add too much, or take away too much, and Jerry Branch is an acknowledged master of the racetrack, a sculptor in efficiency.

It strikes me as we walk from the Harley to the Big Dog, talking about engines and rides, that it is the motorcycle that brings me here today, both figuratively and literally, and although we have more in common than Branch heads and a twin cylinder engine, without the bike I would not know Jim, or many other people with whom I have become friends. The motorcycle is a connection as much as it is a conveyance. It is also, certainly with the American motorcycle, a personal statement.

With the bike, as opposed to an automobile, it is possible to shape the vehicle to match the needs and ideas of the rider, frames can be chopped and stretched, the angle of the front end altered, the bike lowered, the engine modified, the paint customized. Everything is possible and personality is reflected in every detail.

Jim's Softail looks like Jim. It's low to the ground—although he does claim to be taller in a leather jacket—and potentially dangerous, with the Bad Dog megaphone pipes and Arlen Ness drag bars giving it a chopped functional aura. On closer inspection, it also appears to have done a few miles, though like its owner it has been well maintained, which in Jim's case, could be explained by his wife, Linda, a practitioner nurse.

She is currently working and both of his kids are out of the house, so after a careful removal of Nancy's rainsuit, which has luckily remained in one piece, and a tour of his facilities, we get into his BMW and head off to a Greek restaurant. Following the retsina, and slightly loaded, I'm beginning to feel right at home in Buffalo, like maybe I should conclude my trip here and spend the rest of the summer with Jim.

Back to his place and the family's gathered. A few minutes after introductions and I find myself slumped against his sofa complaining of chronic fatigue.

Leave it Jim to come up with an antidote. Possibly the only thing that's still legal and guaranteed to get me back in the saddle. Mate. He has the gourd and bombisha that I presented him with in Amagansett, and a full pound of the bitter leaf.

I watch as he puts on the kettle and fills the hollow shell with yerba.

"Don't let the water boil," I caution.

"I remember," he answers, turning the gourd in his hands to shake the smaller, more powdery leaves to the bottom.

A minute later he removes the kettle from the flame, saying, "I think we're there."

Linda declines to join in—probably because of her medical training—while his eleven-year-old son and nine-year-old daughter watch suspiciously as he carries the water and the accompanying paraphernalia to the crusty, semi-inebriated visitor on the sofa.

The clouds in my head begin to part after my second hit, and by the third my throat feels like it's been ported and polished. I'm sipping through Branch heads.

Then, with no apparent thought between sitting and standing, I'm on my feet, hugging Jim, hugging Linda, thanking them, saying good-bye to the kids, and making my way to the bike.

Jim extends a final invitation to spend the night and I

briefly entertain thoughts of becoming his apprentice, exclusively for the Fox Hunt shoots, after which I'm down the ramp, rolling, turning right, accelerating, another right, following his instructions, straight on to the Peace Bridge, stopping for the border check, and over the Niagara River.

Good-bye Buffalo, good-bye Jim.

Then, just like that, good-bye America.

One mile at a time.

I'm traveling.

THAT DARING YOUNG MAN
(On the Flying Trapeze)

THE QUEEN ELIZABETH HIGHWAY toward Toronto feels like a silk ribbon. The sun has passed its peak, the air has cooled and the Big Dog is gliding along at a smooth eighty-five. The speed seems natural, as if the bike, the condition of the highway, the sun, and the wind have conspired to dictate their own momentum. I'm just along for the ride. There's nothing like this feeling. It is both self-contained and complete, my body and mind working in an easy harmony with the machine. This is the kind of riding that dissolves the tensions in my psyche. There is a spacious quality to the feeling, as if my mental walls have collapsed and there is finally room inside to find perspective and insight without everything closing in and seeming so damned urgent. As if I am outrunning the negativity that is attached to day to day life, discarding it as I ride into a state of relaxation where the most urgent matter is the moment, the now. Riding is a way of finding focus and with each mile the journey becomes more simple, and the task more apparent. All I have to do is ride. To get to

Sturgis, that's my job, and the simplicity of knowing that brings a kind of order to everything else.

There's traffic up ahead and my speed drops from eighty-five to sixty, then down to fifty and by the time I see the sign for Hamilton, I'm nearly standing still. It's rush hour in Ontario and I've been caught, in more ways than one. Hamilton is where my father was born.

The last time I saw him he was clad in a white hospital gown and laid out on a gurney in the Chadwick Funeral Home, in Ardmore, Pennsylvania. It was about an hour before his cremation but the undertaker had waited for me to arrive so that I could say my last good-bye. My dad and I were alone in the room and I remember his face on that day more clearly than I do on any other day in my life. His thinning brown hair, patchy and gray in places and parted to one side, lines that looked like ridges in the sallow skin of his forehead, narrow, deep-set eyes, the deviated septum of his nose and his wide, full mouth which seemed, even in the final sleep, to be grimaced. Without animation everything which had once been handsome seemed enlarged and distorted, like a mask. My father had suffered. It started with cancer in his esophagus and spread to his lungs after which he'd endured the standard western medical torture of chemotherapy and bedside oxygen tanks before being attached to a morphine drip for the final ride out.

I hadn't seen him for a few months and as I looked down at him, needing to feel some kind of connection, I realized that if I had passed him on the street, I would not have recognized him.

"Hello, Scout," I said, trying to reestablish something between us. I had called him Scout since I was a kid.

Starting out as a joke, the name had begun with his grandfather, a wayward soul, who had insisted that Roy, my dad,
addressed him as the old scout. I'd thought it was funny
so I'd borrowed it.

"Sorry I wasn't there for you," I continued, guiltily, staring down at this stranger.

"Don't worry about it, Champ," he answered.

I could hear his voice in my mind as clearly as if he
were speaking to me. He'd been calling me Champ for as
long as I'd called him Scout, and with my life in tatters at
the time of his death, there was a real irony in the name.

*"I wasn't expecting to go so soon either, but what the hell,
it beats paying taxes."*

That made me laugh. My dad could always make me
laugh. In fact, he could make most people laugh. There
was rarely a situation, no matter how bleak, that he
couldn't turn into humor.

I bent down and kissed the cold skin above my father's
eyes.

"See you later, Scout."

It was time to go. I'd come. I'd seen him. It was over.

Then I heard his voice again, in my mind.

"Sure thing, Champ, and sooner than you think."

That stopped me cold. I took another look down at the
dead man on the gurney. Closer. His face had changed,
or more likely my eyes were for that moment perceiving
differently. I was looking at myself.

His message was clear. If I wanted change in my life
there was no time to hesitate. Time was passing, and that
passing time was all I had.

Mohawk's Highway Cruiser never cruised. By the time my
first summer in Amagansett rolled in I was going to be a
father, for the first time, at fifty. Betina, the mother to be,

and I were renovating a house and planning our shotgun wedding for the fall.

Sometimes it has seemed necessary for me to die to one life in order to find another, and sometimes the dreams of that life perish with it. Crossing America by motorcycle, the great dream of Albany, while divorce lawyers were slugging it out, coal fires were burning and my Harley Springer rusted in the courtyard, was by the summer of '96, out of the question. The most I foresaw using my new saddlebags for was toting diapers home from the local CVS.

My needs had changed. I no longer felt the call for adventure, or escape.

Mohawk's bike sat for a year beneath the carport, serviced, and inspected, polished occasionally, with less than two thousand miles on the clock. I rode it into town. I rode it to the beach. I rode it once, with Betina on the back, to visit John in Connecticut, but never further than that. Suddenly, from being an aging boy with lots of toys and lots of time to play with them, I was a family man.

It was the best thing that ever happened, filling a part of me that had been empty, and giving new perspective to old ambitions and values that seemed hollow in the light of my new life. But I did get pangs, and there were the memories.

There was a time during my transition from married man to single man and back again, that my old friend, Bro Si, with whom I have ridden many a sun-baked mile across the Sierra Nevada desert in Spain, decided to clear our heads with a ride through Baha in the middle of June. I rented a Harley from Easyriders in LA (Si had moved there from London and shipped his Heritage) and we took off. Right into Mexico's rainy season. There were some won-

derful mountain roads, winding and lonely, stretches of
beach that ran straight for miles, amazing vistas—between
cloudbursts—but the highlight of the trip, for me, came
just south of Ensenada where we encountered five student
nurses from San Diego.

It was a night of tequila and wild dancing. In fact, inspired by Si's prowess on the floor, I dusted down many
of my own forgotten steps. It was at the height of these
psychedelic contortions that I noticed Bro Si had disappeared. Which was a concern, since he had been complaining of stabbing pains in his lower back, brought on
by a particularly rough patch of unpaved road on our way
into the club.

I scanned the crowded dance floor, then the bar, where
one of the nurses reported that Si had last been seen gulp-
ing a birdbath-sized margarita.

Out to the parking lot. His dusty black Heritage was
still there, leaning patiently on its kickstand next to my
rented Fat Boy.

I began to worry.

El Mambo wasn't a particularly dangerous place, but it
did have a strange contraption hanging on what looked
like twin thirty foot poles in the center of the large, outdoor dance floor. The thing appeared to be some type of
circus apparatus, sort of a cross between a trapeze and a
gallows. I had no idea what it was, or what it was used
for, but it looked ominous. A small circle of people had
begun to gather at its base and instinct drew me toward
them, but before I could elbow my way across the floor
the music stopped.

A hush fell over the club, followed by the recording of
a drum, rolling from six-foot speakers of the surround-
sound system like a clap of looped thunder.

Then silence, as the crowd parted and a beacon of light hit the twin poles.

I still didn't know what was happening.

The drum roll intensifed.

Then, a gasp from the crowd as a dark-haired man, about six feet tall, handsome without being pretty, and harnessed in what looked like a black straightjacket, shot straight up into the air. It was like a bungee jump in reverse. He rose like a star in the night, then dropped like a stone. Rebounding a few times until, finally, he hung there, dangling from the elasticized cord while waving his arms triumphantly to the fans on deck.

It took me a few moments to recognize Bro Si, in all his denimed glory, dangling at the end of the rope.

By the time the applause died down, Tina Turner was wailing "Private Dancer" and the vacationing nurses were gyrating in my direction.

The tequila had been better than a general anesthetic and Bro Si lived to ride halfway to del Cabo, but it was that moment in Ensenada, with him swinging proudly above the dance floor, that I will always remember.

Yes, family life was great but there were definite pangs.

Then came the telephone call from Indianapolis that would put me back in the saddle.

His name was Tom and he had tracked me down through the lawyer's letter which appeared in the Foreword to *Hog Fever*, bearing my family's address and written to to my father in 1965, assuring him that despite charges of operating my Norton motorcycle while under the influence of alcohol, driving recklessly on private property (along a sidewalk while engaged in a race with a milk truck) and having long hair which was a general offense to the community (the judge would not hear my case in court unless I surrendered to a marine-style buzz-cut) that I would probably get off with a suspended driving license and a stern warning.

Tom had dialed 411 to get my parents' home phone number then sweet-talked my mother into giving him mine. Introducing himself to me as a man of vision, a mid-life biker, HOG official and super salesman, he explained that he'd read *Hog Fever* and loved it. This was, however, was no average fan; Tom had a mission in mind.

"With the right promotion your book could have people laughin' from coast to coast. Everybody'll own a copy. You'll be on Jay Leno's show." Words that rang sweet to my ears. I could mix my biking passion with business.

Tom went on to talk about conventions, T-shirts, badges, emblems, and grassroots, in the saddle promotions, all amounting to massive book sales. In Tom's mind, and mine, by the time his pitch ended, an empire was being born. I would become the symbol of midlife biking, the Marlboro Man on a motorcycle, the Celebrity Bro.

I suggested we meet and he agreed to take the next plane to New York.

It was all catching up with me.

WOODSTOCK

THE GRIDLOCK FINALLY BREAKS on the far side of Hamilton. From crawling along at ten miles an hour and inhaling lungfuls of Canadian unleaded, a slight twist of the throttle has me back in the wind, off the Queen Elizabeth Highway and on to Route 403 headed toward Windsor, at the southwestern tip of Ontario.

The sun is setting in the right lens of my clear goggles in bursts of gold, red and purple. The air has a chill. Hard to believe that yesterday when I left the beach, it was a hundred degrees. It suddenly feels like fall. It also feels like yesterday, even today, are way behind me, somewhere on the far side of the Peace Bridge.

I ride through the cool of early evening, feeling alone in the best sense of the word, alone without loneliness. There is no place else I want to be at this moment, no place but on this motorcycle, traveling along this road. There is pure luxury in this experience. I envy no one. I want nothing. I am out of competition, out of the race.

Every signpost has a certain lure—Stratford, Tavistock, Paris—I'm free to visit these places, to pull in and pull out, to stop and eat, to spend the night or to keep on traveling. It's a particular type of freedom, the freedom of the ghost. No one knows I'm here. There are no telephones, no emergencies, no panic. I'm connected only by thought to those that I love. There is exquisite peace in this moving solitude, in which the only sound I hear is the steady beat of the twin cylinder engine.

The sun is just below the horizon and the light is soft, not much more than a glow, giving the leaves of the tall trees which line the highway a golden incandescence. This is the magic time of riding, when I am not desperate to stop and I am not desperate to forge ahead. I'm simply riding.

This feeling continues until the road is dark and first stars become visible in the sky. It is only then that I notice that my body is tired. I feel it first in my shoulders, a soreness in my neck. I'm thinking again, about hot baths and a firm bed, about how much gas is left in the tank, trying to calculate how many miles I've come since I filled up in Buffalo.

I spot a road sign for Woodstock, which immediately conjures images of Jimi Hendrix playing the "Star Spangled Banner" on his LSD-powered guitar. Hard to believe that the great music festival was thirty years ago, but now the name alone seems fated, enough to pull me off the road, even though it's a different Woodstock, and a different country.

The first thing I see as I come down off the connecting road to the highway is a low sprawling restaurant and a brick-fronted hotel. The hotel looks modern and well kept, with parking bays directly in front of the big windows of the groundfloor rooms.

I check in, get my key, and roll the bike to the bay that adjoins my room. Check it for loose bolts, fluid leaks, lock it down, and carry my bin liners inside. A quick survey of my map tells me I've done about four hundred and fifty miles today, which considering my stop in Buffalo, isn't bad. It must be the mate, and I regret not having a traveling gourd.

Then the ritual, beginning with getting out of my boots which feel, having been soaked and dried about five times in the past twelve hours, as if they've been cast in concrete and permanently molded to my feet, followed by a careful removal of the articles from my bin liner. Nancy's rainsuit is treated with a new respect, as are my wife's goggles, which I wipe clean before laying everything out on the bed, like a man on a desert island taking inventory of his possessions, realizing how much he will be relying on them until rescue.

Forgoing the knife fighting drills, along with my grandfather's mirror exercise, I get straight into the espadrilles and out, across the street to the restaurant where I hole up at a side table and become an observer of family life in a small Canadian town. The grilled chicken and string beans are a blur of charcoal and barbecue sauce and I feel myself fading with the baked potatoes. Happy to get back to the sanctity of my room, leaving my clothes in a heap on the floor, I roll back the covers of the king-sized bed and climb in.

The sun is down, the lights are off, my eyes are shut, but my mind is on and my dream is lucid and unexpected.

Back almost forty years, to the lawn behind the cafeteria of Lower Merion High School, with my Cushman Golden Eagle parked in the lot to the side of the building. I am about to engage in my first real fight. My opponent is very angry, and determined. Avenging the rumor that I have sneaked a kiss with his girlfriend at a party. Whether or not I "felt her up" is the real issue and I won't answer so he's threatened to kill me, which leads me to retort that "Nobody can kill me."

He's the co-captain of the high school wrestling team and a known street fighter. I'm a guy who lifts weights and writes poetry. Other than quick flares of temper and giving a few friends bloody noses, I've never had a serious fight. Inside, I know I'm outclassed. I've got that sinking feeling, buoyed up by a stupid pride that won't let me back down.

The contest begins with him dropping into a semi-squat, with arms extended he rushes forward to execute a classic wrestler's double-leg takedown, which I counter—as I'm falling backwards—with a headlock, my one and only grappling move. On my side with him on top, his head trapped between my biceps and my chest, I squeeze as though my life depends on it, which I'm sure it does. For a solid minute he can't break my grip, but it's a terrible minute because the headlock constitutes my entire fighting repertoire, and he's not giving up. In fact, judging by his grunts and death threats, he's going insane. Still, hanging on and squeezing desperately, I try to make him quit. He doesn't and the strength is seeping out of me, until I feel my arms are made of rubber. Then I feel his head moving, slipping out of my vise. I'm losing him. On my back before I know it, with him straddling me, shouting "Nobody gets me in a headlock!" he punches down into my unguarded face, over and over again. He's got a big, thick ring on his third finger and it's leaving indents in my forehead. On and on. I've got to save myself so I roll and struggle to my feet. I can barely see him through my own blood as we square off again. He tells me it's over. I tell him I still won't quit. It's my pride again, even now.

"You're a hell of a tough guy," he says, dropping his hands.

I wake up.

The bedside clock reads 4:13 and I'm back in Woodstock, Ontario, with the Big Dog chained outside the window, but the fight is as clear in my mind as if it just happened. I can almost feel the bruises. The only discrepancy between my dream and reality is that the fight was broken up by the football coach and Dean (the victor) never did tell me that I was a tough guy.

The trauma and humiliation of that event, witnessed by half the high school, pressed up against the windows of the cafeteria, provided motivation for many years. I was terrified that it would happen again, so I armed myself against it. Decades in the gym, eighteen years of karate, sparring with professional boxers, trying to develop a tough shell to protect the kid who got the shit kicked out of him on that playground. Thousands of kicks and punches, thousands of hours given to the rematch in my mind, a long list of injuries, both to myself and those I trained with. Unable to rise above my own ego. Until I began to realize than it was the uncontrolled part of myself that frightened me, the unknown in me, the bursts of temper, like a child's tantrums, and the projections of that uncontrolled rage that attracted negative situations and people like a magnet. With that realization came the first stirrings of self awareness, and the eventual realization that awareness is the heart of all martial arts.

But why all this now? Why this dream?

Perhaps it's the remnants of that uncontrolled child who still lives inside me, desperate for resolve, trying finally to emerge as a fulfilled man. Telling himself that he's a tough guy. Reassuring himself. Propelled by the fear of the unknown, and the knowledge that anything can happen on a long ride, and in this case there would be no John to help me off the motorcycle.

This ride is down to me, and how well I know my self.

The shower feels like a massage, washing the last remnants of the dream from my mind. Bringing me back to the moment without losing the lesson.

The stars are still shining when I step from my room to check on the bike and my breath is a white mist in the air. It's cold but it's clear and the air is pure and clean. I'm going to need that heavy shirt. I'm going to need everything I've got. At the heart if it, riding a motorcycle is also an exercise in awareness. It's life and death in the blink of an eye.

With an apple, a banana, and a bottle of mountain springwater in my belly, I start the engine of the Big Dog at 5 A.M.

On the road before morning light.

DAY THREE

LIFE IS WHAT HAPPENS TO YOU WHILE
YOU'RE BUSY MAKING OTHER PLANS.

—JOHN LENNON

JOSEF

ROUTE 403 MERGES WITH 401 AS THE SUN comes up in my
rearview mirror. The road is wide and flat and the bike is
humming. It's cold in Canada at 6 A.M., but the chill feels
good against my face and I'm dressed for it with the heavy
pullover beneath my leather jacket. I'm riding through
farm country and to my left and right the land is lush and
green.

At this hour there are a lot of trucks making time, heading for the border, which keeps me moving at about
seventy-five miles an hour, a little faster than I want to
travel because the morning is nearly perfect; there is no
fog, no side wind, and the road is bone dry. The sun is a
brilliant gold, warming the air as it arcs upward. I'd like
to slow down and make this section last but the penalty
would be a large metal grill up my rear end.

My alternative presents itself about half an hour later,
just west of Port Stanley. It's a service station with a view.

I pull in, fill up, then ride to the far end of the parking
lot, away from the pumps. There I shut off the bike and

sit, gazing across the lot, across the highway to the fields beyond and Lake Erie beyond the fields.

I feel like a bird on a wire, on top of the world.

"Listen to me. I know what I'm talking about. I'm an old man, I know these things."

Josef was seventy-seven years old when I last saw him, and he often used the old man line when making a point. Standing about five-feet-four in his shoes, with a white Van Dyke beard that made him look somewhere between a satyr and a rabbi, and weighing in at a hundred and ten pounds he was a tiny man who'd led a large life. Beginning as a child prodigy with his violin, working as a frontline correspondent during the first war in Israel (where his wife-to-be had died from a bullet wound, in his arms), he then became a television producer in Hollywood, responsible for the original series of *The Untouchables*. In his prime Josef was a film mogul, fond of dictating memos to a battery of secretaries from his throne, a toilet seat in the bathroom of his London office.

I met him after his empire had crumbled.

"We couldn't have been friends before," he assured me, with a sparkle in his faded eyes that reflected the devil he had once been. "I was too much of a prick."

In fact Josef was pretty well out to pasture by the time he'd read one of my screenplays and decided to produce it. Unfortunately Hollywood, where people are terrified that the age of forty is terminal, didn't want to know about an old man and his dreams.

"Can't get a fucking phone call returned," he complained, a day before finding out that he had cancer in the marrow of his bones.

After all the women ("screwed more beautiful broads than Anthony Quinn") chauffeurs, movie star friends, money, and fame, not to mention memos from the throne, Josef was relegated to a Jewish home for the elderly and infirm on the wrong side of Battersea Park, in southwest London.

I got to love Josef, he became an extension of my own dad, and during my sojourn at Albany, while taking my Saturday bike rides in the cause of two-wheeled psychiatry, I made him a regular visit. Sitting on a folding chair in his ten-by-twelve-foot service flat, with its tiny sink, refrigerator, stove and single cot bed, while wearing his uniform of white tennis shoes and gray sweats, he brewed us a pot of tea. We would usually talk about his life, maybe look at his scrapbooks, showing pictures of him young, dapper and full of himself. Afterwards he'd walk me down to the Springer, gazing at it as if it were one of the fine pieces of art that he had once collected and hung on the walls of his homes.

"Look at that thing," he said, admiring the bike. "Omnipotent. I remember how it feels. I remember."

He wasn't talking about riding. To my knowledge Josef had never ridden a motorcycle. He was talking about what the bike symbolized to him.

"You need that right now," he continued. "That feeling of power, that feeling that you can get on that and go places. You've still got things to do, wonderful things, believe me." Then he turned and looked up at the third floor window of his apartment, with a small terra-cotta pot containing a single green plant balanced on the ledge. His eyes misted over. "I'm dying," he said. "I need to be right where I am, sitting, thinking, praying, coming to terms with myself, trying to make some peace. I don't need to go anyplace else. My daughter and I are finally talking again, after all the years when I was a lousy father, never there, always hustling. Now that's gone, all of it. There's no more money, no more Hollywood, no more power

games, no more bullshit, because in the end that's what
all that stuff is, just bullshit. Relationships are what finally
count, who you've loved and who's loved you back. That's
what you take with you. Believe me. I know these things.
I'm an old man."

Before I leave the rest area I dig into the pocket of my
jacket and find my wallet. Stuffed in the back, along with
my folded British driver's license I keep a small picture of
my wife and son. It's one of those six for three dollar color
snaps taken in a booth at the mall, probably on a visit to
Chuck E. Cheese's. I study the two faces in the photograph, knowing that there's another face in the photo, currently hidden in mama's belly. Two faces, three souls, my
family.

   Josef was right, by comparison: everything else is
bullshit.

DETOURS

TRUCK TRAFFIC HAS THINNED BY THE TIME I get back on the highway, and so have my thoughts. I'm no longer rushing in the same sense I was only a day ago. As my body relaxes, finding its own sense of peace with the motorcycle, my mind follows, gradually emptying. I'm traveling at sixty-five and the world is opening in a rush of sights, smells, and colors while the crisp chill in the Canadian air adds to the illusion of moving through time. I feel that I have been traveling across the seasons as well as the highways, riding from summer and into early fall. Occasionally I pass another motorcyclist going in the opposite direction and we hold up a hand in a static wave or nod a greeting.

My trip has already distanced me from my prejourney fears and the warnings of the armchair warriors, those people who sit around, scared of the things they really want to do, dying slowly and regretfully. At the same time it has begun to distill the mental sludge that accumulates in my own mind from day-to-day living. One of my frequent errors is thinking that I need more than I actually do: more time, more food, more money, more success, more of everything. More is better. The ride has the effect of stripping that feeling away. Get up, get dressed, get on the bike. Get tired, stop, sleep. Gasoline for the engine, food for the rider, a warm bed, dry clothes, a hot shower. It's simple, yet it is that very simplicity that I so often lose in running the race, or playing the game, where the carrot—dangled in the pages of every magazine or flashing across the T.V. screen—is wealth, fame, eternal life, a wrinkle-free face, luxurious hair, and washboard abs.

The uniformed guard at the Canadian border looks at me, then my photo ID, then at the bike.

"You headed to Sturgis?"

It's the first time anyone has asked and his question makes me feel closer to my destination and, by his familiarity, closer to home at the same time.

"Yes, that's where I'm going," I reply.

He hands me back my license, smiles, and wishes me a good time.

An hour later I wish I had asked him directions. I'm so lost I don't even know which state I'm in. I think I may have drifted south, down into Ohio but I'm not certain. It all began with a detour sign on the west side of Detroit, then got worse. One detour led to another and my single roadside stop served only to confirm that my 1989 *HOG Touring Handbook* was severely out of date. So I ride on, along badly paved sections of unmarked highway squashed between a lot of highway cones and veering metal. It seems everyone is lost, cutting in and out, switching lanes without warning, shooting off at exits, and I don't want to stop and lose valuable time by finding out where I am or, worse yet, discovering that the last sixty minutes have been a total waste, so I continue with my blunder, praying that

I'll see a road sign that will tip me off to where to pick up Route 94 west.

The road sign for 94 doesn't happen, although several more detour signs do. By now I don't even know where I'm detouring to, since I didn't know exactly where I was when the original detour began. It reminds me of an afternoon I once spent circumnavigating the nation's capital, with one of America's wonder boys, a corporate tycoon with a Midas touch. Neither of us knew the other very well. We had started out from New York City as a group of ten, then due to various stops for gas, food, or engine failures, had split up. Finally, it was just me and my new and only friend, fully leathered and visored, with Jimi Hendrix belting "must be some kinda' way out of here" from the dual speakers of his tricked out Road King. I was glued to his tail, and kept wondering why everything looked so familiar, at least every half hour or so, as we made a three hour circuit around, and around, the Washington Beltway, but didn't dare interrupt or question his gyroscopic maneuvers, thinking he was too brilliant to be lost, at anything.

Now I've done it all on my own, and it's not half as much fun, because there is no one to blame it on but myself. Yet I continue to ride full steam ahead because somewhere, deep inside, I feel I can't afford the time to stop. The fact that I may be going in the wrong direction is incidental to my need for momentum.

Another detour, another road, getting smaller, another town that wasn't on my map and I admit my error.

Still, it's hard to pull over. Harder still to own up to the fact that I may have traveled a hundred miles in the wrong direction. The implications are enormous. Is this the way I live my life? Veering from highway to highway? What if

I missed the main road thirty years ago and have continued to travel my life by detour? Should I have taken that doctorate in psychology? What the hell was I doing in London for twenty years? Where am I now and where could I be if I had paid attention to my needs and not my whims? Christ, I'll never get to Sturgis in time. I may even be late for the last half of my life. I'll be *seventy-four* when my newest child is twenty.

A signpost for Mishawaka lights the path though this journey into cerebral darkness.

I pull off, onto a smaller more rural road and continue for a mile or so before I spy a service station. It's a cabin-sized wooden structure with two pumps out front and a rusty pickup truck with Hank's Auto scripted on its side, a bit of circa 1941 to augment my current sense of disorientation.

I pull in as if I'm entering the Twilight Zone.

A plump, rather attractive country girl in gray overalls appears from the door of the cabin and walks towards me.

I attempt to make my tone casual so as not to spook her.

"Could you tell me what state I'm in?"

She looks at me as if I may be joking.

"Ohio?" I ask, expecting the worst.

"No sir, you're about five miles outside of Mishawaka in Indiana."

My spirits rise as I unscrew the gas cap. At least Indiana is west of Ohio.

Pushing my luck I continue. "Is that anywhere near Chicago?"

"Just keep going straight, maybe a hundred miles and you'll be right in the middle of Chicago," she answers, handing me the pump. "You want to do this? I'm afraid I'll spill gas all over the paint. My boyfriend's got a Harley and he's always yelling about spillin' gas on the tank, so you'd better do it."

I take the pump and begin to fill the bike.

"You going up to Sturgis?" she asks.

I answer yes, making sure that I don't leave a river of gasoline on the harlequin finish, as she informs me that she and her boyfriend made the trip to the Black Hills last year for a few days. Then she invites me inside for a map reading and a glass of apple cider. Being from New York, where being rude is practiced as high art and the deadline factor causes executives to wear running shoes beneath the cuffs of their Prada suits, I'm already visualizing an ambush. As I follow her into the cabin I'm suffering mental replays of the last act in *Pulp Fiction,* in which Bruce Willis is abducted by Zeek, taken to the basement, and tied up next to the chained gimp in a black leather mask.

We arrive at the counter with the cash register where I hand over five dollars and seventy cents for the gas while she unfolds a road map which makes mine look like a relic from the pre-automotive era. Apparently we're alone, although I maintain a tight-assed Samurai awareness, just in case Zeek busts in.

By the time she has introduced herself as Connie and uncapped the bottle of cider—locally brewed she tells me—I'm feeling more secure, completely out of *Pulp Fiction,* and into something more erotic, probably a B-movie with X overtones, where to the tune of John Mellencamp's version of "Wild Night," which is playing through the tinny speaker of a portable cassette deck on her desk, she locks the door of the cabin and begins a striptease, while I watch guiltily through my wife's goggles.

Nothing like that happens and she's about as straight and friendly as a certified paranoid from New York can handle without valium.

We go over the map until I know where I am and where I'm going. Connie's patient, like a schoolteacher and seems concerned about my apparent lack of directional abilities, finally dismissing me with a complimentary bottle of cider. One for the road.

Back in the saddle I feel as if I've just spent an hour at the feet of the master. My mind, caught speeding again, is back within its limits.

I wave and ride out of Connie's, or rather, Hank's, accelerate to about forty and hold it there, conscious again of the wind in my face and of the beauty of the countryside, ambling on to Route 7 which will connect me with Highway 80 west. My urgency has, for the moment, dissolved, and when I'm certain that I know where I am, I decide to have the cider. As if by synchronicity the perfect resting spot appears. It looks like Graceland, a big, white, Southern-style mansion sitting totally alone in the center of an enormous green field. Complete with columns, an entrance gate, and a long winding drive leading to the front porch. I'm not spaced out enough to venture in unannounced, just enough to pull up beside the iron gates, shut off the bike and remove Connie's cider from my saddlebags.

The sun has passed its peak but it's still warm and relaxing against my back and there are the most beautiful white clouds drifting overhead, like billowing sails.

I feel fine, actually better than fine. The cider is cool and sweet, the sky is blue, the air is warm and I have found that space, once again, where everything inside and out feels perfectly aligned. As if I am exactly where I am supposed to be at this precise moment, doing exactly what I am supposed to be doing, and I couldn't have arrived at this point without the detours in my life, all of them. The detours were crucial, and now I'm in no rush to get anywhere.

Plus, this is Indiana, home of the Colonel.

THE SPRINGER, SPRUNG

TOM AND HIS WIFE Kathy arrived in East Hampton by train. I arrived, to meet them, in my wife's white, '64 Thunderbird convertible. It was the nearest, in length, that I could come to a limo.

The first thing I noticed, after the drooping mustache and red baseball hat, was a sparkle in his eyes, as if we both shared a secret joke, which we did, although neither of us knew quite what it was at the time.

I packed them into the T-bird and headed home where Betina had already cut the limes and spread the salt in preparation.

Kathy was sweet and reassuring, a balanced presence in the midst of a powerful man-to-man talk about horsepower, Harleys, U.F.O.s, the paratroopers—in which Tom had done a stint—and the inevitable fame and fortune that would result from spreading our midlife biker gospel—all of this fueled by multiple margaritas. Then Tom, newly promoted (by me), because of his military background, to the Colonel, was gone. I assumed he'd ambled off to use the bathroom but knew otherwise when I heard the bellow from the fishtails on the Highway Cruiser. I had mentioned that he could ride Mohawk's bike, even insisted upon it, but I hadn't reckoned he'd be on it within the first hour of our business meeting. I got to the door in time to wave him good-bye, watching him depart from our gravel driveway with both cowboy boots dragging for stability.

"Tom just loves motorcycles," Kathy said as he disappeared around the block.

I stood on the front porch as my bike became an echo in the distance, wondering if it would ever find its way back again.

A few minutes later I heard the sound, like firecrackers exploding in a tin can, and knew all was well. Then watched as the Colonel rolled gracefully into the driveway, skid once on the gravel, made a correction with his snakeskin boot and brought Mohawk's bike to rest under the carport, adding a much needed mile or two to the clock.

"Nice ride," he said, hauling his faded jeans off the saddle. "But it's not the Springer."

I knew it wasn't the Springer. At the time of his visit the Springer was banging around England like an orphan without a home. Everybody loved it but nobody wanted it.

"We can't promote the book without the Springer," he explained as we headed inside to carry on with our intoxication.

"I'm selling the Springer," I stated.

"How much?"

I had started at £20,000 (about $35,000) and, having had no interest, dropped to £16,000.

"Sixteen thousand," I answered, settling back into my chair.

His eyes perked up, even his mustache twitched.

"I'll take it."

The moment of truth had arrived and I was reluctant to say yes to what I'd been trying to do for nine months, sell it.

I sounded like I was arguing, throwing up obstacles. "Yes, but the bike's in England."

"We can ship it."

It was easier for me to think of the Springer if it was in a different country. It was the most personal bike I had ever owned. I'd cut my teeth on the Springer, ridden it across Europe, rebuilt it three times, ridden it to Albany, ridden it away from my divorce. It was a symbol of my past. There were memories associated with it that I wanted to leave behind and memories that I would always hold close.

"It will be part of the business," the Colonel reasoned. "You can't just let anybody have it for sixteen thousand dollars. That's giving it away."

It was at that point that I knew I'd made a crucial error.

Correcting myself, I said, "Sixteen thousand *pounds,* not dollars. That's about thirty thousand dollars, plus shipping."

His mustache returned to a full droop.

"Can't promote the book without the bike," he repeated, looking soulfully at the layer of salt on the lip of his glass.

I knew he was speaking the truth, besides he'd touched a nerve. I didn't really want to sell the Springer at all. The problem was, aside from needing the money, I had no place to keep it. The Highway Cruiser was already showing spots of rust from being left outside, and the Springer was impractical. Without more money spent on mufflers and indicator lights, it would never pass a New York State inspection.

The mustache twitched again and his lips parted in a smile.

"Why don't you just ship it to Indy?" he said. "We'll keep the papers in your name, store it in my garage, and you can ride it at the rallies."

The deal was done, even as I heard my wife choke on her drink.

I had just agreed to ship my motorcycle to a guy who lived a thousand miles away and who I'd known for under an hour, but . . . the Colonel and I were in business.

The Springer, shipped by Warr's, arrived in Indianapolis by air, direct from London, England. I was in East Hampton at the time, connected by phone to the Colonel's corporate headquarters, as he and his team of recruits went to work on the crate while I received a blow-by-blow description. Obviously they were attacking it rear end first.

"Nice wide tire," or "love the solid wheel," the Colonel's salty voice would comment down the line as I listened to sounds of exertion followed by boards snapping. "And look at those pipes. Are they three-inchers?"

I would answer as quickly as I could, reliving the entire customizing process in my head as, piece by piece, the bike was revealed.

Finally, with a bang and a snap, the front end emerged. I knew this because I heard the Colonel grunt, cursing under his breath, before he said, "Somethin's wrong with the clutch."

I wasn't concerned because that was the customary response to my hydraulic masterpiece. It had been installed by Snob, motorcycling socialite (hence his name) one-time president and long-standing member of the London Chapter of the Hell's Angels Motorcycle Club. "Gotta be a real man to change gears," he'd challenged, just before I'd had my first tug on the steel lever.

"Pull harder," I advised the Colonel.

Another groan, then success. "Oh, yeah, it does work, just have to have forearms like Popeye to operate it."

A few minutes later and I heard the roar of the pipes, which was impetus enough for me to book a flight.

I arrived at *Hog Fever* headquarters in the passenger seat of the Colonel's Dodge truck with a small crowd of enthusiasts waiting for us in the driveway.

"Just a few people who've read the book," the Colonel explained as we rolled in and stopped alongside the Wells Fargo trailer that he'd leased to tow the Springer to our pending list of cross-country engagements. "The numbers will grow as we get out the word."

Then, as if on cue, the garage door rose like a curtain, revealing the Springer, flanked by the Colonel's Softail and Kathy's Sportster. It was cleaned and polished, reflecting the thousands of copies of *Hog Fever* that were stacked in the background, insulating his walls.

There was also a remarkable collection of antique and vintage pedal bicycles and a long, folding card table, complete with two phones, a well filled ashtray, a squashed pack of Camels and a cowboy hat sitting in the middle.

"Welcome to our corporate offices."

I shook a lot of hands, no doubt repeating the ritual with the same ten people many times over as the evening progressed, and my confidence in the new business grew with every can of Miller High Life.

There was Bill, with his wife Laurie, who worked at the local Harley dealership, and their daughter Jennifer. They were a family who rode together. And Bro Byron, a silent investor in the new corporation, who had formerly been a member of the elite Delta Force military unit and was currently involved in the administration of human organ banks. He was kind enough to assure me of the availability of spare body parts if the need ever arose while I was in Indianapolis. His pretty wife, Terri, promised me he could deliver.

"T-shirts and badges should arrive next week," the Colonel said. "Everything will be together in time for Sturgis."

Sturgis, the magic word, the big rally in South Dakota, stomping grounds for half a million bikers and every major outlaw club in America. I'd read about the wild parties and wild rides in every biker magazine I'd ever thumbed, fantasized about it from the briny waters of my flotation tank in London, but what exactly did the Colonel mean?

"Sturgis?" I asked.

"That's where we're headed," he replied.

And the show hit the road.

TERMINAL

RELAXED, FLOATING ALONG AT EIGHTY in my highway easy chair. Not a care in the world as I cross the border into Illinois, the sun in front of me, and over a thousand miles of road behind. Well, maybe one care. I'm being strangled by the strap of my helmet, not all the time, just when I accelerate to overtake a slower vehicle, which for the past hour has been everyone else on the road. With the exception of the homicidal strap, which I correct by pressing down hard on the top of my lid when overtaking—giving the appearance of a one-armed bandit to the caged victims of lesser vehicles who stare, bewildered, from behind a layer of tinted safety glass—I'm having one of those magic unions with the machine that makes me feel impervious to accidents, danger, pain, or gyroscopic slipups.

Unfortunately ego and awareness are often in conflict, and with barely a slip of the throttle I find myself headed off a ramp with "Detour" printed in bright red letters above it. The next sign reads "City Limits" and shit, I'm going to Chicago, just when I was hoping to circumnavigate the place altogether.

Backing down through the rev range my helmet strap loosens up and I'm swallowing easily, bumping and grinding, as I ride a slalom course around potholes and crevices that I thought were the sole property of New York's Triboro Bridge.

There was a song, way back in the seventies, written and performed by the late Jim Croce. It was about a man named Leroy Brown, meaner than a junkyard dog, who met his end in the south side of Chicago. Well, Jim, I know where you got your inspiration because I'm here on the wrong side of the railroad tracks, under the bridge and bouncing along a road that hasn't been resurfaced since the Great Depression, at ten miles an hour in front of a façade of seedy bars, pool halls, tobacco stores, and a parade of street people who look like they would happily carve the Big Dog up and eat it, along with my espadrilles. Not a friendly face on the sidewalk, it's more like I've invaded enemy turf, even the Timberline is quaking in my boot. Not a place I want to stop and ask for assistance, and I seriously doubt if anyone within my immediate vicinity has heard of Sturgis. The problem is I'm lost, riding deeper and deeper into this concrete jungle, without a single detour sign to guide me.

I carry on like this for what feels like a year, then as my hopes dim and the urgency to urinate increases, just as I am searching for a connection in the manic eyes of a stranger (at least enough to ask him where I am), sitting next to me at a traffic light, blowing black smoke from the exhaust pipes of his battered Lincoln Continental, I see the equivalent of a light at sea, in the depiction of that long, streamlined bus, carrying a fleet of happy campers across the wonders of America. It's the symbol for the Greyhound Bus Company, etched into the big plate glass window of a flat squared building occupying a corner lot,

on the far side of a railway trestle. I'm home, with a toilet
and maps, and employees who are sworn to assist.

Inside, the place is more like a morgue than a way station to cross-country adventure. There are one or two
dreary-looking souls sipping coffee as they sit on long
wooden benches that look like medieval church pews and
a few more who are either dead or unconscious, laid out
with their shoes on and old newspapers covering their
chests. Waitin' for that old 12:09, I suppose. And a woman
behind the desk who seems oblivious to everything, including my brisk entrance and quick disappearance to the
back of the lobby, following signs and jogging in the direction of the rest room.

It's empty and clean, with soap and towel.

Afterward, I'm almost a new man, relatively relaxed and
fast on my feet, at least able to communicate.

"I'm looking for 80 West," I ask the woman at the desk.
Maintaining a respectful tone, sensitive to the prostrate
bodies on the bench behind me, apparently in the initial
stages of rigor mortis.

"Straight ahead," she answers without looking up from
her bus schedule.

After all this inner turmoil I can't believe I've actually
been going in the right direction.

"Pardon me?"

She looks up without focusing her eyes, points her finger in the direction that I've been riding and repeats.

"Straight ahead about three miles. You'll see the signs."

I want to ask, "Do you promise?" but manage to limit
myself to "Thank you."

Taking one last look at the gathering, and meeting some
of the glassiest eyes this side of Madame Toussaud's
Waxworks, I depart.

The promised three miles turns into five, then seven,

and the south side is not getting any friendlier, plus I'm tired. I've been at it for about ten hours since morning call in Canada, and I'm ready to quit, although the one dilapidated hotel, or rooming house, that I ride by, offering a single bed for nineteen bucks doesn't quite entice me enough to surrender.

Another mile and the detour signs miraculously reappear, posting the way back to the main highway. I follow them with tunnellike vision, petrified of missing my escape route.

Finally, I'm back out on the highway, going seventy with the wind in my face and my mind stuck in the Greyhound Bus Terminal. I think of those people, then I think of myself, sitting in a chair, looking out the top story window of my English manor house, staring glassy-eyed at the falling rain, wondering what had become of my life and where it had all gone wrong. Waiting for the next Greyhound.

I'm tired out and my body has begun to tremble, as if it's cold outside, even when I know the late afternoon temperature is in the eighties, but at least I'm back in the land of the living, on a road that I know. I'm certain a motel will appear sooner or later, but a public rest area catches me first and I pull in, ditch the bike and lay down in the shade of a giant tree. Eleven hours, pretty much nonstop, and I can hear the rumble of the bike in my head and feel the vibration in my body as if it has become a permanent state of my being. I stare up at the leaves, dancing lightly in the gentle breeze, as my body feels like its growing roots, and those roots are going down, into the earth. My eyes seem to focus in a different way, for the moment uncluttered by thought. I see a hole above my head, straight through the branches and up to the sky where there is a single patch of turquoise blue. The rhythm of the leaves and the solitary blue, like a fine polished stone, capture my entire attention and my next sensation, as I go off to sleep, is that I am rising up, out of my body, floating on a pillow of warm air, going up to meet the blue. I catch myself, muscles jerking, as I jolt upright. A moment later I regret not letting go, because just for that moment I could fly. It was fear that stopped me, of the unknown, the unusual, of being in a place without anything familiar to hang onto.

I stand and brush the dirt and grass from my jeans, walk back to the bike and climb on.

Next exit, I vow. I'll get a room and a bed. That's all I need.

There is something soothing in the sound of the engine as it starts, low and throaty. The bike rides easily down the connecting road and out onto the highway, as if it too has rested. Accelerating to seventy-five miles an hour before I'm even conscious of its speed, as it becomes an extension of my reality, I'm beginning to get a true instinct for this bike. It's as if every nut and bolt has become connected to every fiber in my body and our collective wills are transporting us to South Dakota.

It is nearly eight o'clock in the evening when I see a highway sign with the symbol for a bed on it. Three miles, it says.

Minutes later I'm pulling in for the night.

The motel is a long, thin two-story structure that looks like a battleship, with a large satellite dish mounted on a pole from its roof. Situated across the road from a gas station and within earshot of Route 80, I'm too tired to notice its name, only that the ground floor rooms have large enough concrete porches to roll the bike to the front door and chain it to a post. Good enough for me.

I notice my hand is shaking as I pay the $39.95 and the fellow behind the desk informs that there's a restaurant

about a mile down the road. The idea of getting back on
the bike and going out to eat is beyond my comprehension.
Dinner is going to be a Power Bar. I've still got two left,
both oatmeal, which seems like a rare and priceless delicacy. My mouth is watering as I make way for the privacy
of my chamber.

My own little piece of roadside paradise is the size of a
prison cell, with a double bed taking up most of it. In front
of the bed there's a table and a television. I don't bother
to get completely undressed, boots, jacket, and pants off
will do as I lie down. The passing cars on Route 80 continue to drone. I can't imagine being out there. Without
the bike beneath me, with all its untiring horsepower, I
feel as weak as a child. The drone continues as I unwrap
dinner and force my teeth through the honey-coated shell.
Doesn't taste quite as sweet as I imagined, in fact it's taking more energy than I've got to chew it. I hear the screech
of air brakes and the bellow of a truck's horn and I wonder
if I can sleep with the noise. Maybe a little television,
sucked down by that huge satellite dish. I get hold of the
remote and hit a button.

"A white sport coat and a pink carnation—"

I recognize the song and the voice, although I haven't
heard either since I was about ten years old.

Images form from the flecks of gray on the screen and
a jukebox appears with a couple dancing in front of it, the
guy wearing white buck shoes and the girl in a frilly party
dress, while Marty Robin's sweet tenor tells me he's all
dressed up for the dance.

I remember myself, wearing penny loafers, black chino
trousers, a white oxford cloth shirt, and a red bow tie,
pushing my eleve-year-old partner around the floor of the
elementary school gymnasium while a dance instructor
named Walter, as thin as a rake in his mohair suit and red

bow tie, crooned above the music, "Right, left, slide to the middle, that's it, the fox-trot is so easy to do."

I hit the power button, Marty's voice fades to memory, the set goes black, and I pass out.

DAY FOUR

EVERY EXIT IS AN ENTRY SOMEWHERE ELSE.

—TOM STOPPARD, PLAYWRIGHT

CELL MATE

THE OMINOUS HIGHWAY DRONE of last night sounds like a lullaby as I wake up with the rising sun streaming through the open blinds of my window. I'm in exactly the position that I was nine hours ago, on my back, arms stretched out, feet slightly spread, sort of a crucifix without the cross, which means I haven't moved all night long. Which is saying something for a man who has been cited, by his wife, for complaints of insomnia and aggressive nocturnal behavior (blanket theft). I'm a little stiff in the lower back and shoulders, but otherwise rested and ready to go, even my injured knee feels stable as I walk to the front door, open it, and check to see that the Big Dog is still chained to the post. The dreads of last night, when the trucks and cars sounded like war tanks, are replaced by an absolute yearning to get on the bike and join the parade. On top of that, the Power Bar seems to have softened with bed rest, probably because I was lying on it, and virtually melts in my mouth as I down it with a bottle of springwater and hit the button on the T.V.

It's Marty again, singing. Still dressed up for the dance,

but as the lyric lilts, someone else has stolen his dreams and he won't be going to the high school prom after all. At the end of this tragic verse a toll free number bobs up on the screen and an announcer's voice assures me that this and a collection of other fifties' classics can not be found in record stores anywhere, and are available only through this ad.

Marty continues to croon in the background as the honey-throated announcer repeats the 800 number and the song is imprinted, at least for the next ten hours, like a skidmark on my brain.

I forego a shower and get my gear on to the rhythm of a fast fox-trot—one, two, slide to the right—

Go outside—Slide to the bike.

Make sure everything is locked down tight—

"I'm all dressed up for the dance—"

The first full-blown *Hog Fever* gig took place on the Fourth of July. It was centered around a card table, twin chairs, a stack of books, and a *Hog Fever* banner, which the Colonel had commissioned for the launch of our enterprise, unfurled and mounted on twin poles above our heads.

Byron was there, with saddlebags that I assumed contained body parts and the Springer, polished till it glowed, sat like a hopeful magnet in front of our pitch. From the theatrical luvvies of London to the Indiana State Fairgrounds, the Springer and I seemed to be joined by umbilical cord. I kept looking at it, somewhat amazed that life can change so much. When I had built the bike, and written the book, I lived in another country, with another wife, and had a very different life. There had been an isolationism about my existence, a certain elitist quality to the grand manor house, the Bible-spouting Filipino maid who, when not on her knees praying or on her toes stealing coins from bedside tables, spent hours ironing my socks, T-shirts, and underpants, and the full-time driver who met me at the airport whenever I traveled.

The motorcycle had been a bridge to the real world, and the card table at the fairgrounds was about as real as I'd been for a long time.

We were set up, along with a hundred other vendors, for the official HOG rally. HOG stands for Harley Owners Group and, in England, following a spell as road captain for the Chelsea and Fulham Chapter—replaced after a disastrous attempt at leading a group of twenty enthusiasts down one of the entrance ramps of a motorway, after mistaking it for an exit, in the pouring rain—I didn't have much to do with HOG. I've never been a group person and my fascination for the bad boy image of motorcycling made it difficult for me to accept the clubby, cappuccino atmosphere of the King's Road warriors and the black and gold HOG patch, made to resemble an outlaw insignia and sewn on to shiny leather jackets reserved for weekend outings, while the two-piece Armani suit and Gucci loafers were temporarily stashed inside the closet.

I wanted something more committed. I devoured books about the Hell's Angels, started hanging around Snob's workshop—long enough for him to wreck the Springer during a test ride and rebuild it—getting to know him in the process, and several of the other Angels who were generally on tap. Not a hanger-on, the term used to define someone looking to prospect for the Club, I was, at that point in my life crisis, looking for other worlds that were real and self-contained, as far removed from the pathology of Ravenswood as I could get. Extreme worlds. Outlaw bikers, boxers, and tattoo artists, provided a counterbalance to the theatrical land of the Darlings, which had become superficial to me.

In America, I found the HOG groups to be much more diversified along the socioeconomic scales and their members to be a generally harder bunch. At least that's how it appeared to me at the Indy Rally.

While the Colonel prowled the perimeter of our traveling book store, I sat at the table, pen in hand, waiting to hit the best-seller list. During the course of the afternoon, I watched as his sales technique evolved. It began as a subtle, even cautious, attempt at welcoming the onlookers, who initially gave us wide birth.

After a couple of hours and no sales, I noticed that his voice grew louder, then he began a back slapping technique, followed by a full arm wrap as he dragged prospective buyers to the table with, "Hey, you want a good laugh?" That line, augmented by, "You gotta' read this book!" was developed and honed in the following months, and finally, along with the droopy mustache and a Camel Light, became the Colonel's trademark.

We started to sell, but more important, we started to meet people.

And everyone we met had a story, from Suzy Q. who recently had won the Miss Iron Butt competition by logging 11,000 miles in the saddle in ten days, to Sandy, who had, since her husband's death (on a motorcycle) in April, been on the road, all by herself, riding from state to state, rally to rally, camping out and living rough. She had built houses for a living and I remember her handshake to be dry and strong. She was honest, independent, and without self-pity. When I asked her why she was riding, she answered simply, "to think things through."

The more the Colonel hustled, the more the cast of

characters grew. There was Tom, the ex–Navy Seal, who spent sixteen years on the rodeo circuit and had twice broken his neck, and was now spending more time riding his Harley than bulls, because "it relaxes me." And Georgia who had recently dropped her bike while it was still running and in gear, only to suffer what Chris, the Indiana State trooper and part of the precision riding team, termed the gyroscopic effect, as the fallen motorcycle chased her around the street—embarrassing, sure but also dangerous.

By the time Stuart, one of the original group who I'd met when I first arrived at the corporate office, arrived with his van, Rita, stocked with several pitchers full of its namesake, the Colonel and I could see the pot of gold at the end of the rainbow. If we could sell forty books at the Indiana HOG rally, we could sell forty thousand at Sturgis. "You wanna' good laugh?"

That night, with our motorcycles parked in a squared gridlock in the center of Indianapolis—due to the fact that not one of the 1,500 party-going HOG members had had the foresight to realize that the closer we parked the motorcycles the harder it was going to be to move them, until it became impossible—and while we waited for the bikes closest to the perimeter to leave, the Colonel and I, exhausted from a day of vending and well lubricated from multiple visits to Rita, walked arm and arm down Main Street, assessing our day's performance, talking about our midlife career prospects—or crisis, and laughing at ourselves till we cried.

These are wonderful miles; when the bike purrs contentedly and the road runs smooth and straight, with the sun beating down and the flat lands of Illinois spreading like parched yellow wings to either side, opening up a space in my mind. I'm flying through a portal in which I can see clearly, where I've been and where I'm going.

Indiana seems like a place halfway between yesterday and tomorrow, the Springer a reminder of my personal struggle for an independent identity, and the Silver Bike as the butterfly emerging from the chrysalis.

All this self-revelation is taking place to the tune of Marty Robbin's "White Sport Coat," which is playing over and over again in the back of my mind, turning my life's trials into a music video with a toll free number. Pretty soon, drifting at seventy miles an hour in the backdraft of a long haul trucker, and closer by many miles to heaven, my thoughts blow out like a candle's flame, and I start to sing along.

Just at the high point of the chorus, as I'm belting out the words "white sport coat" and inhaling in preparation for a smooth and soulful "pink carnation," I notice what appears to be a bruise in the blue above my head. It's a cloud, but a particularly ugly one, followed by another, and another.

The temperature drops ten degrees in the space of thirty seconds and my voice segues to silence.

No, it can't rain, I tell myself. The Midwest has been having one of the worst droughts in years. Rain was not in the forecast.

Another five degree temperature drop and the big blue sky looks like it's been covered by a big, flat brown lid. It's getting dark, and all at once I'm cold, hungry, and out of gas. I throw the petcock to reserve and look for a station.

It comes up about five miles later, just as I cross the Iowa border and the first drops of rain start landing like water balloons against the top of my bare head.

I pull off the road and into the station, which is almost an exact replica of Hank's place, minus Connie and the apple cider. The other difference is that there are six

Harley-Davidson motorcycles in line at the pumps,
equipped with saddlebags, windshields and, I assume,
bound for Sturgis. The rain is still sporadic, although the
drops are the size of 9mm bullets, and the evil, purple gray
sky appears to be about a stone's throw above our heads.

I park in line and listen in as the service attendant informs the group, obviously traveling together, that nine
inches of rain has fallen in the past six hours and that
there is severe flooding up ahead.

"Roads are impassable in some places," he warns, as
water bullets pelt my cheeks with increasing rapidity.

"Doesn't look good at all," he continues, as if any of us
have much alternative but to ride on. "Wouldn't catch me
out there on one of them things," he adds, eyeing the bikes
while spilling a half pint of gas over the black paintwork
on the tank of the new Road King. The gas is soon diluted
by the rain and the rider, staring up at the sky and shaking
his head, seems oblivious to it anyway.

I look up, then down the narrow stretch of God forsaken highway that runs cross-wise to the main road and
see nothing remotely resembling a hotel, in fact nothing
resembling anything but flat land, a single old wooden
barn and a few scrawny head of cattle, all lying down—a
sure sign of a big storm, my grandmother used to say.

"This is gonna be a real bad one," the pumper of gas
and doom concludes. "Could go on for days."

I'm getting that hopeless, lonesome feeling when a hefty
woman on the back of the Road King, who looks somewhat overinflated in her square-shouldered set of black
fringed leathers and a full faced helmet that resembles a
huge white bubble, with its visor open, says loudly, "We're
bikers, we can get through anything."

I watch as the group pulls out, then fill my own tank,
roll the bike to the corner of the lot and step off long

enough to drag the rainsuit up and over my soaked blue jeans and T-shirt. Then I tug my leather jacket on and get the helmet from the back of the bike, followed by the goggles.

The next few miles are not pleasant. The rain is falling, which makes it slippery and cold, but the real threat is the sky. I can't remember ever seeing such a sky. It is dark and thick with clouds, layer upon layer of purple and gray, like a shroud.

I notice that the cars and trucks coming toward me, heading east, look as though they've taken a beating, windshield wipers flapping on high speed, mud and grit splattered over their lights and grills, and stern, strained faces behind the wheels.

Another mile and further on, there appears to be a dark veil hanging in front of me. I ride through it, into highway hell. Rain so heavy that it weighs like a second suit of clothes on my body, filling my boots and smacking my helmet hard enough that I can feel it like tapping fingers against my head. It's no longer a question of getting through but getting out of it, as I try and stave off the idea that it really could go on like this for days.

I spot an underpass and have a moment of hope, until I see that the entire length of the sheltered shoulder, on my side, is a line-up of motorcycles, with not a single space available. I ride beneath it, glancing to my side at the squared, inflated lady in fringed leather, minus her bubble hat and with a decidedly worried look on her round face. I remember her words, "We can get through anything." *Well, maybe not.*

Onward into the darkness, with trucks pushing from behind, a force nine gale in my face, my helmet strap loose and cutting a ridge into the underside of my jaw, wiping my goggles with one frozen, sodden finger, while hanging onto the bars with the other hand, and trying like hell to think positive thoughts, the best of which is that this, like any torture, is temporary.

Whatever happened to the white sports coat and the pink carnation? It seems like a lifetime ago.

Then, as if my subconscious, driven by prayer and need, has made it materialize, I see the underpass with the lone Sportster sitting beneath it, the ancient mariner hunched in the corner, puffing on a cigarette, smoke billowing like an aura of white cotton candy around his head, and plenty of room for me.

With a careful pump on my front brakes I slow down and ride on to the hard shoulder of the road, the ten-ton semi who had been mercilessly riding my tail creates a hundred-gallon splash as he roars by, and I'm there, coupled with my new cell mate beneath the concrete bunker, exchanging tales of doom and receiving a stern warning that he had once been sentenced to six and a half hours in a similar location, freezing his ass off, with night closing in. Ten minutes later, I'm wishing like hell that I had a windshield and struggling to pee while watching what feels, at the moment, like my only friend—although we never exchanged names—join the hiss of the highway, as he disappears like a mirage in the vaporous smoke from the steaming wet macadam.

STURGIS, IN THE VILLAGE

FINALLY, BLADDER EMPTY, GOGGLES DRIED AND WIPED CLEAN, several shuddering glances at the sky, which now seems low enough to reach up and touch, and I'm back in the saddle and out on the road, miles behind the ancient mariner, following him into a sea of rain.

It's funny, not "ha ha" funny but ironic, that despite the fact that if I open my mouth I'll wind up sucking down large amounts of water, that this downpour could last for days, and that I may be riding like this for the rest of my journey, I begin to relax. Not to the extent of a relaunch of "White Sport Coat" but at least to a general level of acceptance.

There is a distinct humility factor to doing an enforced sixty miles an hour in a deluge, with the constant hiss of truck tires from front and behind as a reminder that any lapse in concentration could result in being ground into something resembling a Big Mac with chrome, when visibility is limited to the dirty spray from the vehicle directly ahead and the motorcycle no longer feels like the agile jungle cat of the highway but rather a turtle without a shell. The level of awareness required during this type of riding makes time irrelevant. Minutes pass, maybe hours, but it's always now, and it's always wet.

The Mississippi River, which I can see on my left, is a wide gray churning mass, swollen and angry, threatening to spill over its banks and flood the main street of Davenport, Iowa.

The last and only other time time I was this close to Davenport, I was holed up in the basement of a house on the outskirts of town, waiting for a tornado to pass. The Colonel was huddled beside me along with his wife, Kathy, Stuart, and the Colonel's sister, who lived there. The Springer, along with the Colonel's Softail (its tank now adorned with several air-brushed, turquoise Indian feathers) and a thousand copies of *Hog Fever* were stowed in the Wells Fargo trailer and parked in the driveway, hopefully not in direct line with the storm. It was my first tornado and memorable moment, since we were in town to participate in Sturgis in the Village, the brainchild of a former member of the Green Berets who had licensed the name Sturgis in an entrepreneurial flash of brilliance.

Sitting down there in the dark, listening to the special storm team track the tornado on the citizen's band of the public radio station and worrying about my $51,000 motorcycle (add crating and shipping from England to the list of customized parts) I wondered if this, after only one event—the HOG rally in Indianapolis—was the end of our empire.

Fortunately the tornado never touched down in Davenport and, after our sojourn in the basement, the clouds parted and the sun sent a cascade of golden rays down upon the Wells Fargo trailer.

The following morning we were setup beneath a canopy

on Main Street, with the Springer parked in front of our
pitch, the banner unfurled and flapping in a light breeze
above us and my books stacked in front of me like the
Egyptian pyramids.

"Hey, you want a good laugh?"

The Colonel, resplendent in a new suede fringed jacket
reminiscent of Billy in *Easy Rider,* was patrolling the
street, using the wraparound arm technique to spread the
gospel.

Unfortunately, although many eyed the Springer and
were met by a reflection in the polished chrome of my
New York smile, which was a cross between an embarrassed grin and a pained grimace (refined through many
years of standing behind my ex-wife at theatrical openings
and cast and crew screenings of her television epics), nobody ventured close enough to lay hands on a book.

The Colonel's wife, Kathy, had already likened our enterprise to a carnival act and although Stuart assured me
that we were in fact involved in a grassroots marketing
campaign that would pay off in spades, I wasn't totally
convinced. At fifty-one, I wondered if I had the years left
in me to move our pitch from the street corners of Davenport to the late night television talk show circuit.

"You gotta' read this book."

I finally sold one, to the Colonel's sister.

After that, we sat and watched the crowds walk by as I
began to wonder what percentage of the biker population
actually read anything other than *Easyriders* magazine.

The Colonel, carney man in the making, knew from my
attitude that he had a potential situation on his hands.
There is nothing like a temperamental star on a sweltering
day in Davenport, so as I lowered my eyes and studied my
cuticles, pretending to be occupied with anything other
than schlepping my unwanted wares to the basically dis-

interested passersby, the Colonel disappeared. Which really pissed me off. Even Stuart, with his grassroots philosophy and calls for patience, couldn't bring me out of my slump.

Then I heard his voice, like a raspy cigarillo.

"You wanna go on T.V.?"

The Colonel reappeared from behind the tent, carrying a couple of "Sturgis in the Village" T-shirts, one of which was extended in my direction as an offering of appeasement.

Was this my big shot on Leno?

"Talked to Sneaky Pete and he's got us a spot on the local news show," he continued. "They want the Springer on, too. We gotta be ready in an hour."

The next half hour was a whirlwind of organization. First, we put the finishing touches on my wardrobe with a genuine 1953 cutoff denim jacket that I had purchased, while under the influence of several bottles of merlot, from a Ralph Lauren vintage clothing representative for the bargain price of $200. It was so vintage that it hung on me in shreds and looked like a faded blue rag, but after my inebriated indulgence I was determined to get my money's worth, and wore it at every opportunity. Then we coupled the Wells Fargo trailer to the Colonel's truck and after a three man polishing frenzy, loaded the sparkling Springer inside. Ready for the big time.

Which was a small studio up a hill, off the main drag of town.

Sneaky Pete and I were to be interviewed, while Stuart and the Colonel hovered behind the cameras, videotaping the proceedings, and offering their moral support.

The newscasting team was male and middle-aged, dressed in matching black funeral suits and, between them, at least an inch of face makeup, giving them the ruggedly tanned appearance of old cowhide. One of the team also served as the station's weatherman, when his presence was not required for celebrity-bro interviews. Once in position, sitting in opposing card table chairs in front of a black, shroudlike backdrop, with the Springer parked casually to the side and the weatherman straddling it, we were given the ten second countdown to showtime.

I don't think the news team was actually prepared for the interview, or attached any particular weight to its relevance, and the initial questions were mostly aimed at the local boy, Sneaky Pete, and how he'd come up with the idea for "Sturgis in the Village."

I felt under a certain obligation to promote the book and could feel the pressure, specifically in the armpit region of the vintage Lauren, and hoped I wasn't producing any unsightly rings. All the while watching Sneaky Pete elaborate on his plans to make his show a yearly event, expanding the territory by bringing in big bands, more vendors, and more motorcycles. Was I ever going to get a chance to speak?

Finally, after rehearsing, in my mind, all the possible questions that I could be asked, and the multitude of witty answers that I would respond with, one of the behind the camera technicians made a gesture with his right hand that suggested he was using his extended index finger to cut his own throat. A signal that time was up.

In one last and dramatic gesture the weatherman, astride the Springer, turned towards me for the grand finale.

"And what's something like this worth?"

The cameras closed in my face as my lips puckered and my mind went blank. After all, I had dropped a small fortune into rebuilding the bike three times. I had shipped it halfway across the world. It had been the black hole in my credit card, an integral part of my life and my divorce. How could I put an honest price on the Springer?

The weatherman waited as the sweat stains etched deep into the forty-year-old denim armpits of my vintage Lauren, no doubt doubling its resale value.

Finally I blurted, "Probably a lot more than your house."

I admit, it was not the most tactful reply but it was not intended as an insult, simply as a bit of irony on a hot day in Davenport, but it quickly changed the tone of my guest appearance and the weatherman, mildly red in the face beneath his quart of tan, countered by making a quick segue into the latest jackpot figures in the Iowa State lotto, all the while glued to the saddle of his house.

After our appearance on the news show, watched by at least six of the three thousand people at the event, we shifted a few more books, notching up a grand total of sixteen copies by the end of the day.

Well, sixteen books in the Village was the equivalent of sixteen thousand at Sturgis, the real thing, or so the Colonel predicted.

FATE

PAST DAVENPORT AND ACROSS THE FLAT WETLANDS of Iowa, hugging the slow lane of Route 80 and accepting the possibility that the rain will never stop.

The only positive thing that has happened since I left the underpass is that I'm no longer cold, which I attribute to the fact that since my clothes were soaked when I put on the rainsuit, its plastic skin has held in my body heat and warmed up the water, effectively turning the rainsuit into a wetsuit. Either that or I'm in the first stages of pneumonia, delirious, and don't know it.

There are times when the rain is so intense that I consider pulling over again, but inevitably on these occasions, someone else, riding a motorcycle, sloshes by in the passing lane, giving me just enough inspiration to continue. I've seen bikes with side cars, with small trailers attached, with their riders communicating by two-way radios, but I haven't seen another without a windshield, which makes me feel somewhere between a diehard and an idiot. Developing a Sturgis or Bust mentality.

A tank of gas later and the rain hasn't stopped or let up

for a minute, but now, instead of being the only bike at the pump, I am more likely to be one of ten, all bound for South Dakota. Without a doubt, I'm casting eyes on some of the weariest, grimmest faces this side of the Mason–Dixon Line. Communication is minimal and mostly non-verbal, a nod of the head here, a wave of a wet gloved hand as another biker pulls out from behind the pump and slops back across the connecting road towards the soaked gray ribbon, westward bound.

As I pull out, three more bikes pull in behind me, all Harleys, and though I'm roughly eight hundred miles from Sturgis, it feels as though I have become part of a procession, some sort of pilgrimage. My apparent reason for going is to meet up, once again, with my Silver Bike, but there's more to it than that. The more I ride, the more I become aware of my ulterior motive; this is an exercise in transition, a catharsis for all the accumulated crap that has lodged in my brain and influenced my thoughts.

The first time I saw my first wife, all of her anyway, she was sitting naked, with the exception of a thin coat of silver paint, on a Triumph Bonneville. I thought she had a lot of courage, small and shiny in the spotlight, up there in front of a theater full of people. The play was the old standard, *Lady Godiva*, but with a modern twist. In this version, Godiva rode a motorcycle, not a horse.

She was an actress.

I was American, twenty-eight years old, long-haired, and waiting at the stage door—after a hasty invitation, extended by her during a dance at a friend's wedding. Professionally, using the term loosely, I was an entrepreneur, importing cowboy hats, belts, and boots from Mexico, but I wanted to be something else, maybe a rock singer, maybe a shrink, or maybe a writer. Anything but a boot salesman.

Her invitation to see the show extended to us spending two weeks together in a small bedsit above the theater in Coventry. I extended the honeymoon by inviting her to accompany me on a buying trip to Mexico. It was a trip that included, for her, emergency gynecological surgery in a Mexico City hospital, with the added treat that no one spoke English, and the standard practice was to get the patient on the operating table and into the stirrups before there was any hint of using an anesthetic. For me, it was dysentery. Bad enough that at one point the hospital asked for an address to send my body. While we were convalescing, all our clothes and possessions were stolen from my Ford van.

Following Mexico, there was no place left to go but the altar.

Our relationship was always volatile, but in the next eighteen years, during the cease-fires in our daily skirmishes, we had some great laughs, and saw each other through many changes and over many hurdles. I tried to be a rock singer, and failed, made considerable money in property and then in a strange twist of fate, in which a movie I had written died in preproduction, but not before the script had been sold to a book company, I wrote my first book.

My ex-wife, after complaining about the stupidity of the script during an acting job, went home and wrote her own. It was rejected, but an anonymous T.V. editor scribbled "great idea" in the margin behind one of the subplots, so she reworked the subplot as the main theme and came up with one of the biggest British television dramas of the decade.

Years later, unhappy as to the way various companies had produced her subsequent scripts, we discussed alternatives.

"We could start our own production company," I suggested, even though I realized it would add to her already 14-hour days at the word processor and practically would insure I'd never see her again. In spite of that it seemed a natural progression.

I hired a friend from LA to run La Plante Productions. Ironically, she was the same friend who, two years later, suggested I book an appointment through her in order to eat lunch with my wife.

The company became my wife's company, and my friend became her one woman P.R. firm, social secretary, bodyguard, and general appendage, even doing a fair imitation of her voice over the telephone.

I felt abandoned, resentful of living in the shadows, but I also understood that I had been instrumental in creating this world in which she thrived.

I had helped her become the person she needed to be.

And in a strange twist of fate, she completed me.

BIKE NIGHT

THE LAST THURSDAY OF EVERY MONTH WAS BIKE NIGHT at the Hard Rock Cafe in Picadilly, London.

It was a poser's paradise. Everyone came to park their paint jobs and display their ink. Bikers got in without standing in line and the entire downstairs of the Cafe was pumped by loud rock music and awash in American beer.

The last time I went, I was living at Albany and in the middle of my divorce. I elbowed my way through the denim, leather, and cigarette smoke in hopes of spotting a familiar face.

And there she was, bent over the bar, trying to pitch her voice an octave higher than Meatloaf singing "Bat Out of Hell," in order to get a glass of whiskey. I recognized her posterior immediately. In fact, I had even had a hand in the choice of the saddle on which it rode, during a period when, as friends, we had personalized her Harley Sportster.

Inspired by this sight, I pushed deeper through the throngs and made it to within shouting range, which was about two feet to her left.

"Hi!"

There was no reply and I became self-conscious. Maybe she hadn't heard me, or maybe my reputation had been was so tarnished by my ex-wife, who, by then, had informed everyone within earshot that the insanity that ran rampant through my family had finally infected me. Or maybe I was uncomfortable because this particular lady was my soon-to-be ex-wife's script editor and I was way out of bounds.

"Over here!"

The whiskey—I knew it was whiskey because she always drank whiskey at Ravenswood, my old home—came and she picked up the glass without looking around. Meatloaf had died down and the inked, barbed wire biceps that had been a flesh barrier between us had hoisted his glass, dislodged his riding chaps from the bar stool, and sauntered away, so I took over his position.

It wasn't just the feeling of being ignored. By now, following months of solo journeys on the bike, hours in the Japanese bath, and a few force-fed insights inspired by a rush of blood to the brain while standing on my head in the tatami room, I needed someone else to confirm my existence.

"Remember me?"

I'd lost a few pounds since riding out of fat city but I hadn't changed enough to be unrecognizable. I was starting to get angry.

"What's the matter with you?"

Finally she turned. Her answer was muffled, but my ears, able to decipher the words of drunken voices wafting up to my futon from Saville Row at 3 A.M., picked it up.

"You're putting me in an awkward position."

I scanned the faces behind us and to the sides. Nobody looked particularly sinister. In fact, with all the shiny leather, silver-capped cowboy boots, and studded belts, it looked more like open night for auditions for the Village People than a bikers' gathering.

"Why's that?"

I met her eyes; they were deep brown and very kind.

She smiled.

"Are you forgetting where I work?"

"This has got nothing to do with work," I said.

Her smile ebbed.

"Do you want to take a ride?" I asked.

The expression on her face changed, suggesting I had just asked for a pants-down boogie on the edge of the bar.

"I'm with a friend," she replied, searching the crowd behind me for rescue.

"Not tonight, another time."

"Yes. Well, maybe, some other time," she answered as a lithe, mousy blond appeared next to her shoulder. The friend, I supposed.

Not waiting to be introduced, or toe tagged, I stood up. "I'll call you," I threatened.

The truth was I had always respected this person. She, unlike the others in the ever increasing legion of my ex-wife's followers, seemed to have her own life and her own identity.

Outside the Hard Rock, on the sidewalk, milling with onlookers, new arrivals, and an acre of chrome and steel, I ran into an old riding buddy, one of my few visitors at Albany. He was bent over his Heritage, seemingly examining the saddle, and I wondered if he was having a quick toot before entry into the din, but as I walked closer I saw that he was merely adjusting his scarf in the mirror.

"Digas!" I yelled, an abridged version of "meatball" in Spanish. It was a nickname that he had acquired during a road trip we'd taken to Spain.

Our conversation lasted long enough for the beautiful scriptwriter to reappear with her friend, in the company of some biking moguls.

I'd been in New York when she'd been hired, but my wife had spoken of her in glowing terms, although even then the description had sounded like a sales pitch.

"You'll really love her, just your type, South American and dark haired, skinny, just like you like them. And she rides a motorcycle."

It had sounded more like dating game than an introduction to another employee of the growing empire.

Stranger things were yet to come, when too busy to attend numerous functions that were relevant to my own work, she insisted I take the South American instead. I felt like I was being pawned off, but if that was the case I couldn't have chosen better company.

Now I intended to take it a step further, but given the sensitivity of the situation, I wasn't exactly sure how to go about it.

THE RATH OF IOWA

FORM FOLLOWS FUNCTION, AND AFTER FIVE HOURS OF RID-
ing underwater my body seems to have mutated. My hands
no longer seem to grip the handlebars by the use of bone,
flesh, and muscle but have merged with them in one solid
connection while my body feels as though it has turned to
liquid and seeped down, adhering to the saddle like wax
dripping from a candle, while I navigate as much by faith
and intuition as by sight and sound. The really unusual
thing is that I am, in a strange, reptilian way, enjoying the
ride.

The land to either side, just yesterday parched brown
and screaming for rain, now looks like it's drowning, with
huge glassy pools spreading out, over the grass and brush.
The trees, trunk deep in water, stare at us, their limbs
extended, leaves bowed and dripping, unable to offer refuge to the human procession as it passes by with the
steady rumble of gas-powered machinery, churning the
rain on the highway into a dirty bath.

I imagine my wife and son. They should be in Crete
now, maybe swimming in the Mediterranean or basking in

the Greek sun. I feel strongly connected to them, maybe by virtue of the water all around me, but more likely because I feel they are in the right place, and so am I. I want to be here. Need to be.

Time passes, or maybe it doesn't while riding in the now, but the temperature is dropping along with the rain and I am becoming aware of little things, like the burning in my shoulders, the emptiness in my belly, and the fact that I am riding in the slow lane and being passed by the same vehicles that I passed an hour ago. I'd hoped to make Sioux City by nightfall, then finish my trip with a long ride into Sturgis tomorrow, but I haven't even hit the junction for Highway 29, which means I must be at least a hundred miles shy of my mark. A hundred miles when I'm fresh seems like a sprint, but now, with fatigue catching up and overtaking me, it's more like a trip to the moon.

I keep my eyes peeled—which is difficult with a membrane of muddy water over them—for an exit. Any exit will do.

The first I see is a sign for Council Bluffs, which sounds impressive enough to lure me off the highway and onto a small road. Figuring that there has to be a great hotel in any place with a name like Council Bluffs. I imagine myself in a luxury suite, with a whirlpool bath, a firm bed, and room service. I don't give a damn what it costs, my plastic will stretch, and I feel I've earned it. Tonight I'll eat extravagantly, maybe a steak, a salad, and a bottle of red, and I'll sleep like a log in my king-sized bed.

The further I ride, the harder it rains, and the darker it gets.

Still, no Council Bluffs, but in the distance, which now equates to anything over ten feet in front of me, I spot a sign for Missouri Valley. Better yet, I see a motel, or something close enough to build my hopes, advertised by a yellow marquee with the words Rath Inn printed in black letters below a logo which reminds me of a large umbrella. The Rath is a single-story L-shaped structure featuring a large courtyard with another building, identified as the Oehler Brothers, a stone's throw from it.

It looks good to me. Very.

Plus, every downstairs room at the Rath has a small porch and two posts holding up the roof above, so the bike will be dry and chained when I pass out. The only problem I see as I rumble into the lot, with the rain playing Pearl Harbor in double time against my helmet, is that it appears that every biker who has ridden past me in the last ten hours was headed for the Rath. There doesn't look to be a single room without a mud-covered Harley, or two, in front of it.

I sit in the courtyard, engine running, hopes drowning, as I scan the main strip of Missouri Valley. There are two other motels, the Days Inn and the Super Eight, but from my limited visibility it appears that each is as infested with Harleys as the Rath, so I decide to try my luck.

Riding to the nearest end of the L, to a corner room with OFFICE printed on a shingle above the door, I park the Big Dog and unfold my body like a sheet, wet from the washing machine.

Phrases like "Hey, I'll pay anything. Name your price. Look, I'm begging you," pass through my addled brain as I twist the knob and enter the office to the sound of a buzzer that reminds me of a game show clock signaling time's up.

A fellow, wearing a white T-shirt, jeans, long hair, and a gold hoop in his left ear, smiles as he looks at me from behind the desk. For some reason, I feel about a foot tall. Not only have I wrinkled, but I believe I may have shrunken in the wash. I feel inferior to my host, maybe because he's absolutely dry and I'm absolutely soaked, or maybe because I'm prepared to beg him for a room.

"You going to Sturgis?" he asks, his tone a hundred shades friendlier than the sky outside.

"Yes. If this rain ever stops," I answer in a tone that betrays my quivering testicles.

"Tomorrow," he says. "It's supposed to be clear."

I'm not sure if I believe him or not. It's hard to believe that it will ever be clear again, but it doesn't matter anyway, not right now. What matters is tonight.

"Have you got a room?"

He looks doubtful, then down at his guest registry as a pretty, dark-haired woman in overalls walks in the back door. She's holding a mop and waste bin in her hands. I'm holding my breath, when, looking over at us she says, "105's open. I just made the bed."

The man looks up. "You're lucky, that's the last one I've got tonight."

I do feel lucky and grateful. The idea of getting back on the bike and back on the highway seems beyond my physical capabilities. Still, I push my luck an inch further.

"Have you got a few bin liners you could spare?"

She answers quickly as if my request is a common one at the Rath.

"How many do you need?"

"Three or four would be great," I reply.

"The laundry room is right next door, and your room is one over from there. Why don't you get your bike out of the rain, then stop by?"

I don't even start the Big Dog back up. It rolls easily to the porch beneath the roof, wet and filthy, with the engine still steaming. There, I chain it up and kiss it good-night, feeling as indebted to it as I would to any close friend who'd just pulled me from the raging waters of a flood.

The rainsuit has ridden up, beyond the top of my boots and I figure I've got an inch of water in each one. They make a soft, gurgling sound as I quick step my way to the laundry room, not wanting to be late for my appointment.

There, the lady from the office presents me with six black beauties, every bit as heavy and durable in texture as my originals, then laughs when I offer to pay for them.

"They come free with the room," she says.

Which, at thirty-nine bucks, I reckon is a hell of a deal.

With my new collection of bin liners clenched in my hand, I hug the building tight against the rain as I make my way to 105.

I love hotel rooms. All kinds of hotel rooms. I think my affection dates back to early in 1970 when with $800, a guitar, and a sleeping bag I set off for Mexico. My quest was spiritual, although it did involve the ingestion of a variety of psychedelic plants and mushrooms, and after a suitable degree of enlightenment I ended up on the U.S. side of the border, hitchhiking my way across the post-hippie American dream. My journey lasted months and during that time I was hosted by such establishments as the Salvation Army Mission in Santa Barbara, California, the Hari Krishna temple of Berkeley in San Francisco, and a small jail cell in Provo, Utah (the charge was vagrancy). Plus an evening held at gunpoint beside the road just out-side Las Vegas by a couple of snaggle-toothed desperadoes who intended to use me as a front in order to hitch a ride and steal a car, then panicked when a wild-eyed cowboy stopped, stared indifferently at their shoddy firearm and demanded gas money before we set foot in his rose-colored Mercury. It was a robbery in reverse. I produced a ten dollar bill and took off with the cowboy, while the gun-slingers remained marooned in Vegas. That, along with many nights in my sleeping bag, praying that a couple of good ol' boys with a six pack in their belly and a pickup truck, didn't decide to stop and play football with my head, convinced me of the value and security of a small room with double locks on the door. Stretching my cash for nearly a year, I occasionally treated myself to any hotel brave enough to take in a barefoot, long-haired man, wrapped in a blanket, and carrying all his possessions in one hand. I stayed in some classics and, as long as they were clean, loved them all in one way or another. They provided security, space to exercise, play my guitar, think and sleep, and sometimes, a hot shower.

Room number 105 at the Rath Inn is a highway man's dream, something from the Jack Kerouac *On the Road* era. Everything is faded, from the pastel flowers of the wallpaper to the pink woolen blanket that covers a double bed which takes up most of the space inside the floral walls. There is also a large television and a white metal unit that looks like a combination heater—air conditioner. That's the thing that grabs my immediate attention. There is just enough room to walk between it and the bed and it takes hardly any time to figure out how the control knob works and to speculate that if I leave my boots on the grill all night, with the heat on and the fan blowing, they'll be crisp by morning. The idea of warm, dry boots gives me great peace of mind. Enough to speculate on dinner with the Oehler Brothers, but not without a few considerations in the department of my wardrobe.

Once out of the rainsuit I notice that my jeans have dried in certain areas, like around the knees and thighs, although areas around the ankles, seat and the crotch, where the denim is made thicker by pockets and belt loops, are still fairly saturated, as are my undergarments, but hell, I can live with that for another hour. What I can't tolerate is the water in my boots, and that's where I've been blessed with a particularly good idea. So it's off with the offending cowhides, which takes an extraordinary toll on my biceps strength and gymnastic abilities, rolling around on the bed, breathing hard, trying to get the soaked leather to clear my soaked sock, before dumping the water down the drain in the shower stall. And then for that moment of brilliance as, with today's socks hurled into the wastebasket and a brand new pair pulled from my saddlebags, I slip one on my right foot. It feels warm, soft, and absolutely luxurious. It would be sacrilege to try and jam this foot inside one of my drenched boots, and I have no intention of pirouetting into the Oehler Brothers in my espadrilles, so I place my stocking foot inside one of the new black bin liners, then slide the plastic-encased foot into my cowboy boot. It enters with a satisfied "pop," and the sensation of heat is instantaneous, like a steamy sauna. Then, with the other foot bagged and in place, and the tops of the bin liners stuffed inside my jeans, giving me the appearance of having enormous if somewhat misshapen calves, I put my soggy leather jacket back on and head out for a night of dining, using my helmet as an umbrella as I run the twenty yards across the parking lot.

It's about nine o'clock and the crowds are either gone, holed up inside their rooms watching weather reports on the television, or they know something that I don't about the Oehler Brothers, but I have no trouble in finding a leatherette cubicle with a panoramic view of the vacant street, the yellow sign for the Rath, and the pounding rain. I also have a clear shot of my nose, which in the reflection from the window looks large, red, and raw, like a distortion in a Christmas ball, its protrusion enhanced by hair so wet and matted that it has molded like a flat, fringed helmet to my head.

My wife has often accused me of being vain. It's true.

I exercise religiously, watch my diet—at least at home—
comb my hair, and bathe frequently, but there is a difference between the way I am now and the way I was ten
years ago. Not only has the discipline of yoga—less aggressive and very mind-body oriented—entered into my
regime of weights and boxing, but my main motivation is
not the mirror but the kids. I'd really like to be around
and in reasonable condition to see them grow up. I figure
I owe them, my wife, and myself that much. In fact maybe
the beauty of late fatherhood is the loss of a certain kind
of personal vanity, and the understanding of mortality and
the brevity of life, for all of us.

And maybe one of the reasons for this ride is to be alone
with this understanding, to know it as a plain, simple
truth.

Vain? I wish she could see me now, in all my sun-baked,
rain-soaked glory. With my bin liners bursting the bottom
of my jeans and my nose lighting up the menu as my re-
cessed eyeballs squint to decipher the small print without
my forgotten reading glasses, finally settling on a delicacy
in the "specials" section, steak teriyaki. I think briefly of
Amsterdam and the Thai chicken salad, and my vow never
to order anything that doesn't originate within a hundred
miles of the restaurant I'm ordering it in, but I'm curious.
I've never even heard of steak teriyaki.

The waitress is polite and patient as I pretend I can read
the rest of the day's specials before asking for the teriyaki
and a bottle of water.

The request for the water, when there's a perfectly good
glass of the stuff sitting right in front of me, coupled with
my ravaged appearance, seems to spook her. She informs
me that they don't sell bottled water, just soft drinks or
coffee, and that the steak teriyaki will take about ten
minutes.

I wait patiently, occasionally glancing at the reflection of my nose in the window, telling myself that it can't be mine, must be some type of distortion caused by the overhead lights.

The steak teriyaki arrives right on schedule, along with a can of Diet Pepsi, and I dig in. Contrary to other Japanese cuisine, generally marinated in soy sauce and seasoned in saki, ginger, and sugar, the Oehler teriyaki has its own unique taste, not quite Japanese, in fact not quite like anything I have ever tasted before. More like a vinaigrette marinade seasoned with salt, with a bottle of ketchup subtly placed on the side.

Dinner has a sedativelike effect and by my last sip of Pepsi I'm nodding off at the table, barely able to calculate the tip for the waitress as I fumble with my wallet before waddling to the door.

Can't wait to get out of these bin liners.

The promise of clear skies in the morning seems about as distant as Crete, as helmet held in both hands above my head, ankle deep in water, I charge into the Iowa night.

Back to 105.

Behind the locked door and into the floral sanctuary, out of what feels like a body suit made from a hundred pounds of wet cement, with my boots smoking on the grill, my nose cooling down, and my mind fading to black.

DAY FIVE

IT IS THE CUSTOM OF THE CHINESE TO KEEP
THEIR COFFINS IN THEIR HOUSES WHERE
THEY CAN BE SEEN OFTEN. IN THE MIDST OF
LIFE AND HEALTH, IT WOULD BE GOOD FOR
US IF WE WOULD OFTEN THINK OF THAT
HOUR THAT WILL FINISH OUR DISCIPLINE
AND FIX OUR DESTINY.

—PUBLIC SPEAKERS LIBRARY

EAGLE

SOMETHING'S BURNING. It smells like rubber with a hint of steak teriyaki and it's coming from the foot of my bed.

There's smoke.

My boots are on fire.

I'm up and dekinked in a single blast of adrenaline, rescuing my Spanish leathers from the blaze and tossing them to the floor.

They're hot, steaming, and curled up at the toes, resembling twin Venetian gondolas. They also appear several sizes smaller than when I last took them off.

While I ponder my latest catastrophe and shut off the heater and fan, I venture a peek through the blinds and up at the sky. It takes my eyes a few seconds to adjust, and my mind a few more to quiet down and acknowledge the fact that I'm looking up at the stars, like pulsing white diamonds. A blanket of stars.

I forget my shrinking shit kickers long enough to amble to the door, unlock it and walk, stark naked, onto my front porch. There's nobody outside but the Big Dog, and we're familiar enough with each other by now that I don't feel self-conscious. The low flat line of the Rath's roof casts a black silhouette against the night and the dozens of motorcycles, all locked and tethered, look like great, sleeping steel horses. I feel like I am the only person in the world, the only one to know that this moment exists, as if I have entered a vacuum in time, a solitary cell in my own mind.

The night is cool and silent, the air has been distilled by the rain to an exquisite perfume, and the stars look close enough to touch. They have color, twinkling in shades of pale blue, ruby, and yellow-white while the Milky Way runs like a white ghost train from one horizon to the other. The spectacle silences my mind.

I would have ridden this far just for this feeling, of absolute peace.

It lasts until I see a light go on in a room, directly in front of mine, across the courtyard, and fearful of being discovered as the phantom nudist, I retreat.

Back in the room, I check the clock beside the bed. It's 4:45 A.M. Time for a shower, a change of clothes, a good look at the bike, and a lot of riding.

Everything goes according to plan, except for the boots. They actually are smaller than they were before the fry-up. It turns into a royal tussle on the bed, lying on my back, legs in the air, pulling for all I'm worth. Until, once again the bin liners come to my aid, and I pop into position. Still, it takes a few hard stomps against the floor to get the toes of my feet to flatten out the toes of the boots. Then, in yet another inspired cerebral burst, I use the Timberline to trim along the edges at the top, cutting off my artificial calves and ensuring myself some legroom.

At 5:15, I'm clean, my pulse has returned to normal—following my scuffle on the bed—and I'm inspecting the Big Dog for any loose nuts and bolts. It's as tight as my boots.

The Oehler Brothers looks closed and I'm not hungry anyway. The only thing in the world that I feel like doing now is riding the bike.

Out of the parking lot, the headlamp throws a solitary beam of yellow gold against the ebb of night, and the exhaust cracks the stillness of the air.

As I depart the Rath, I feel as if with each stop and each mile, I'm leaving things behind, discarded feelings from my past life, memories, pieces of the puzzle that no longer work in the whole. Replacing them with parts that are alive and vibrate with a different resonance and vitality. I feel lighter inside as I ride up to the intersection, and to the sign for Route 29, which is a straight run north to Sioux City, then into South Dakota, and on to Sturgis.

Just as the sun begins its climb above my right shoulder, making yesterday's flood seem like a lifetime ago, I see a smaller side road, running off to the right, narrow and unmarked, and lined with lush green grass and trees.

Slow down. There is the most wonderful scent of flowers all around me. I look and find them, yellow and blue, growing wild in the field, along the narrow road.

I lean the bike to the right and twist the throttle, headed for nowhere in particular.

There is not a car, truck or bike anywhere and I have this feeling that the world is still asleep and I may be in the middle of its dream.

I ride on without any sense of time, alone in this dreamscape. Through a small town, past a general store, a small cafe, and a fire station.

The sun is higher now, warming the air as it unfolds against my skin. I smell the wet grass on the wind and the sweetness of the flowers, as the tires of the motorcycle grip the asphalt and the bike winds its way around the gentle curves, straightening as my hand pulls gently on the throttle.

Another turn, another tree-lined country road, a tractor ploughing a field, the bluest sky I have ever seen. Light so clear that it makes the colors of the grass, flowers and trees shimmer with the greens, yellows and blues of a sur-real painting.

Then I see it above me, drifting in the sky, so big that its wings block the sun as it circles. I think I know what it is, but I'm not certain. Pulling the bike to the side of the road, I shut off the engine to watch the silent dance above my head.

On Eastern Long Island, we have ospreys, fish-hunting hawks with wingspans of three or four feet. The bird I am watching looks twice the size of anything I've seen on the island, and instead of flapping its wings the way the osprey does, this bird sails through the air, with hardly any move-ment from its dark, feathered wings.

I have never seen an eagle in flight, not before this mo-ment, and as the great bird soars in circles above the green field, less than a hundred feet above my head, I feel both a sense of awe and a touch of fear. This bird is as big as I am, and so powerful that the slightest motion of its wings allows it to sit almost still in the air above me. I feel that it could swoop down and lift me from the bike. Yet, as I watch the creature circle, able finally to make out the golden feathers of its neck, my sense of danger turns to one of respect.

There's a tension in my stomach as the circle tightens and the golden eagle descends, coming closer.

I feel connected by a cord, stretched taut and about to break. Nervous in the way I would be in a situation of physical confrontation.

Then, in a single breath, the eagle drops from the sky.

Impact is accompanied by a fast, sharp chirp, like a burst of oxygen forced from the diaphragm, and I don't know if it's the eagle or the animal clutched in its talons that has made the sound. I can't see clearly, because the animal's head looks smothered by the feathers of the bird's underbelly and its body is hanging loose and still, probably broken by the weight and power of the attack. I watch as the small lump of dark fur with its dangling legs is carried higher and higher by the great wings. Until the golden eagle, carrying its prey, is no more than a speck in the western sky, leaving me alone on the highway, feeling a strange and deep relaxation, as if all the tension in my body has been released by witnessing this single, natural act.

I also feel privileged, as if I've been given a lesson, something so simple and direct, that for a moment, my mind has nothing to talk to itself about.

I sit in silence.

Then start the motorcycle, self-conscious of its sound against the landscape, as if to disturb the atmosphere is to disturb my own tranquillity. But the sound of the engine seems natural, too, and riding feels good. The bike is my wings.

Riding till the road intersects again, and I see a sign for Route 29, north to Sioux City, then I'm back in the procession, headed to Sturgis.

BOSS HOSS

MY JUDGMENT MAY BE IMPAIRED, or maybe it was an hallucination, but something just roared past me that looked like a motorcycle on steroids. Sounding like the V-8 engine of my first car, the '57 Ford convertible, after I'd swapped the stock muffler for a glass pack.

I look down at my speedometer. I'm doing eighty, the Iowa landscape is pancake flat, covered in green-brown grass and thick bush, while the wind has picked up. It's blowing hard enough to give me the sensation that I'm careening down the highway at about a forty-five-degree angle, and that a steady series of invisible waves is pounding relentlessly against my right side.

Still, examining motorcycles in motion, bike spotting, has become a preoccupation in the past couple of hours. I've seen just about everything that rolls, from a Honda Goldwing pulling a Volkswagen Beetle on a tow, to a W.W. II Harley, featuring a sidecar with a bull mastiff in the passenger's seat, wearing a red scarf and dark glasses, but this is my first sighting of one of these monsters.

I look ahead. The giant bike is still in the left lane and

quickly becoming a speck along the gray-white highway.

I twist the throttle and the Big Dog jumps instantly to ninety as I whip out and begin to overtake a white Chevrolet minivan that I've been contentedly sitting behind for the past half hour, resting in its backdraft and using it to break the headwinds.

I'm doing a hundred by the time I'm side by side with the van and I can see its driver, a dark-haired blur wearing thick framed Clark Kent glasses; there's a little boy's face pressed up against the backseat window. He's wearing a red baseball cap and waving at me but it's all very fast and I'm not about to pry my hand from the open throttle to wave back, but for a moment, I think of my son Jack, and look again at the speedometer. It reads a hundred and ten.

"Is that bike hot?" he asks every time I come home from a ride.

"Yes, it's hot," I answer him. "Be careful, don't touch it."

"You be careful, too, daddy."

I am careful, cutting back in front of the minivan, with the wind so strong that unless I hold onto the bike I'll be blown sideways to the soft shoulder of the road, and onto the dirt and loose gravel.

The memory of Jack's face haunts me, pulling me back from the thrill of the chase and into thoughts of responsibility and fatherhood, but the road ahead is smooth and clear of cars, there's not a cop in sight, and the added speed seems to cut through the wind and stabilize me.

At 115 miles an hour I'm gaining on the monster.

The numbers on the Big Dog's speedometer peak at one twenty, then there's about a one inch gap till the needle hits and stops on a small red pin. By the time it does this I feel like I'm running headlong down the funnel of a tornado, with my body hunched down against the tank.

I'm a hundred yards back when I see the rider's head

bob down, and I figure he's spotted me in his wing mirror. Then I'm right on top of him. Pulling to his left side and slowing to match his cruising speed of one hundred and ten. He looks over and nods, seemingly relieved to see me, probably because he was expecting the law.

He's a big guy, like a bull riding a bull, with a black leather jacket and matching hair, cut tight to his head, wearing wraparound *Terminator*-style sunglasses. His face is wind burnt and wide but with the hundred plus air lift, that forces his skin tight to his bones, its impossible to make out his features.

I eye his motorcycle. It features a small aerodynamically designed windshield, a huge yellow and red flamed gas tank and an eight-cylinder, 350 horsepower Chevrolet engine. The rear tire belongs on a car. Although the Terminator has personalized his bike and the brand name has been removed, there is only one company that manufactures anything as testosterone inspired as this. It's Boss Hoss from Tennessee. I remember the Colonel taking a test ride on one and claiming, amidst complaints that the giant engine scorched his crotch, that once he'd opened the throttle the Hoss was the fastest bike he'd ever ridden.

The rider looks over at me again and accelerates a little bit. It's not so much a challenge as an invitation. I twist the throttle to stay even with him. We go from 110 to 120, which he holds, and it is as if he has just opened a door to me, inviting me inside his world of speed and power, to the place where he and his motorcycle live, a place in which the landscape to either side is a blur and the only reference point is the straight line of the highway, dead ahead.

This place is very quick and death, I realize, would be equally quick. But with the Hoss not more than fifteen feet to my side I feel somewhat protected, as if I have a guardian angel with white walls, and a V-8. My late friend Josef was always talking about feeling omnipotent, in his youth, and maybe this is what he meant. We are definitely kings on this road, riding side-by-side, blasting across the wide-open plains like there's nothing else but the wind in our faces and the combined roar of the engines.

By the fourth car that we pass, flying by them as if they are parked, I glance down at the speedometer and notice that the needle appears to be welded to the red pin. That observation has the disquieting effect of eroding my feelings of indestructibility. I'm thinking again of bumps, cops, and animals running in front of us—cars cutting across our path. Dangerous thoughts at over two miles a minute.

I look over at the Terminator, catch his eye, attempt a smile that causes my lips to spread like a quivering mass of parched Jell-O across my teeth, then back off on the throttle, watching as he roars ahead and continues smoothly along the highway like a leather clad Buddha, practicing seated meditation.

After that, 90 miles an hour feels like a jog and at eighty I'm pretty sure I could jump off the bike and walk. Then the motorcycle's engine begins to cough and sputter, forcing me to reach down and throw the petcock to reserve as I look for a gas station.

MISSOURI BREAKS

I'M STILL SUFFERING THE AFTERMATH OF THE HOSS, with an overflow of adrenaline that's causing my hand to tremble as I fill the tank, spilling gasoline over the purple flames, then wiping it dry with my glove. It's time to take a rest, get something to eat, drink some water, lay back, and relax. I look past the gasoline pumps and beyond the station's small wooden office building. I see nothing but flat, sun-scorched earth and hear nothing but the wind, whistling through the telephone wires that line the road.

The attendant looks young, twenty or twenty-five, and he's sipping Coke from a can as he devours a well-thumbed issue of *Penthouse*. He takes my six dollars and twenty cents without a word then continues his life inside the pages as I walk back to the bike, climb on, and hit the starter button.

The sound of the engine carries on the wind.

I look over. The station attendant is watching me, his eyes alive, as if the thumping of the big metal heart has awakened something inside him. Maybe it's the notion of escape from his windowed box, or perhaps he sees a vehicle to the air-brushed beauties inside his magazine. Maybe he rides a bike and has never seen one like mine before. I believe I detect the look of curiosity on his face, as if a rare bird has unexpectedly landed and is about to fly away again.

He stares another few seconds then, unexpectedly, gives me a thumbs up.

Even here, in this void, the bike is a connection.

I nod my head, smile, and rumble from the lot.

Back on the road and I can see the white minivan with Clark Kent at the wheel in my rearview mirror. I look down and note that I've dropped to seventy, which I've come to accept as my normal cruising speed.

I wait for the van to overtake me, wave at the kid with the baseball cap, and slide in behind it like I'm crawling into a rope hammock for an afternoon siesta.

I let Clark and his white van with its "Good Fathers are Good Men" sticker on it guide me all the way through Sioux City and into South Dakota, where they pull off at a Burger King and I keep rolling.

The sun is bright and I reckon the temperature to be somewhere in the high eighties. I judge this by my nose. At one hundred and above the incineration factor is so great that no matter what level of sunblock I use I still run a throbbing beacon by late afternoon. It's untouchable. At ninety and below there's the usual crater effect, caused by open pores, sticky ointment and road dirt, but at least I can touch it, which I do now, predicting that it will be relatively cool—mid-seventies by sundown.

Between yesterday's flood, today's wind, and my quick lesson in humility, provided by Boss Hoss, I know I need a break, but now that I'm in South Dakota and only about three hundred miles from Sturgis I have an urge to push on and make it by nightfall. However, for the moment, I

have lost the euphoria of the ride and my mind keeps drifting to the hot bath that will ease the muscles of my neck,
which feel like they've been inlaid with pins and needles.
Oh, yeah, and an air-conditioned room with curtains
drawn against the sun, and a hard mattress to straighten
the evolving curvature of my spine.

Next exit, I promise.

Then, as if superglued to the saddle, I continue to ride
past every exit sign for another hundred miles, all the
while promising myself that I'll take the next one.

The day's ride has now become an exercise, and with
each exit I'm forcing another repetition, telling myself I
can keep going, turning pleasure into pain.

Finally I see a sign that reads, MISSOURI RIVER. SCENIC
OVERLOOK. PICNIC GROUNDS AND RESTROOMS. 1,000 YARDS.

I love water: oceans, bays, ponds, lakes, rivers, even
swimming pools. Water relaxes my mind, and the idea of
sitting on the banks of the Missouri, eating the last of my
Power Bars while sipping from a cold can of vending machine iced tea, seems like heaven.

I slow down, not giving my other mind—the Sturgis or
Bust mentality—any excuse to shoot by the off-ramp.

The engine sounds throaty and grateful as I ride up the
rise leading to the overlook. The parking area is large and
mostly deserted, except for two cars, parked up by the circular building which I know (because I've been in several
just like it in the past week) will house a large wall map
of South Dakota, pinned with state parks and historic
monuments, and the public toilets.

Depositing the Big Dog by what appears to be the detached back of a house trailer in the middle of the lot, I
head for a dirt trail, marked by signs promising the scenic
view of the Missouri.

It takes a few minutes to climb to the top, but once there the view is magic.

About five hundred feet below, the Missouri winds through the green valley like a long, brown snake. But the river is not the main attraction. Not today. Today it is the rumbling chain of metal that captures my eyes. Hundreds of motorcycles, maybe thousands, forming a continuous procession, crossing the bridge along Route 90, all headed for Sturgis.

I watch them for a while, then I lay back against the warm ground, with my legs slightly spread and my arms stretched out to my sides. The air smells like a delicate mix of dried grass and honeysuckle and the sun is a warm blanket. Within seconds my eyes are closed and my thoughts have slipped back in time.

TRADER VIC

THE FIRST TIME I ARRIVED in Sturgis I was sitting in a small, prop-driven airplane, on a connecting flight from Denver, with my motorcycle helmet resting between my legs. The plane was full with passengers, mostly male, and almost all of them were carrying motorcycle apparel in one form or another. I felt like I was part of a military operation, maybe an air drop. The ride was bumpy and my conversation was limited to a young lady, singular in that she lacked any form of bike-related gear, squashed in the seat beside me.

"Where are you going?" I asked.

"Sturgis," she replied.

That took me by surprise. She was dressed more like a secretary, in a blue cotton blouse, skirt, and trainers, than a biker.

"For the rally?"

"I live there," she answered.

That explained it, a civilian.

"What do you make of this?" I asked, motioning to the

leather jackets, long hair, and heavy boots which filled the cabin.

"Oh, we have a lot fun this time of year. That's when the place really comes alive. My mom and dad rent out the house for the week and we all move in with my mom's sister in Rapid City, but me and my friends like to dress up. You know, in blue jeans and cowboy boots and stick on a few tattoos, the kind you can wash off. We hang out in Sturgis and make believe we're bikers."

"Have you ever ridden a bike?"

"No," she answered as we hit an air pocket, dropped a few feet and settled with a bump that sent a wave of soda over the lip of the clear plastic cup in front of her. "But it's got to be more fun than this."

By the time we'd landed, I'd promised her a ride on the back of the Springer, imagining that I'd see her again. Strurgis was going to be just one, big happy family.

The Colonel, Camel at half ash, looked slightly confused when he met me at the airport in Rapid City.

"Lot of people here," he commented after we'd exchanged greetings. "It's bigger than last year. There's almost half a million."

I didn't understand the implications of his facial expression or remark until we were inside his truck and making our way, slowly, to our rented accommodations in Rapid City. The highway was a lineup of motorcycles in both directions. Every configuration of two-wheeled—and some three-wheeled—vehicle was present. There were stock bikes, custom bikes, and bikes that looked as though they had been tossed together from a basket full of spare parts. There were riders wearing their outlaw colors over tattooed bodies and faded denims, grannys on bikes (as advertised by their T-shirts), and riders whose shiny new leather jackets and fringed riding chaps looked as though they'd just popped out of the Harley dealer's gift box. The distinctive roar of the V-Twin engine was as much a part of the environment as the flat plains and spectacular vistas to either side of the highway.

The Colonel's single complaint during our slow ride into Rapid City was that the sheer weight of the Wells Fargo trailer, loaded with our two bikes and three thousand books, had forced him to travel the entire twelve hundred miles from Indianapolis at fifty miles an hour, and consume an enormous quantity of gasoline.

"We're gonna' sell a lot of books," he predicted as we pulled into the driveway of our new home. I did, however, detect an element of desperation in his tone, probably inspired by the amount of money it would take to break even on the gasoline it had taken to get here, or the amount it would take to get him home again.

Our hosts for this extravaganza were Trader Vic and his beautiful wife, Rachel, a congenial couple who, like the rest of this part of South Dakota, were happy to give up their bedrooms to two strangers on bikes, if the price was right. In fact, instead of moving out of their home, they had simply moved down the hall, giving me the master bedroom, complete with bearskin rug, four poster bed, and shared bathroom, while the Colonel was stationed in the converted basement, an enviable spot because of its privacy.

Trader Vic had an entrepreneurial twinkle in his gray eyes and a voice—jazzed by the fact that bikers drop about a hundred million bucks in Sturgis during bike week— which crackled with deals, from concession stands offering spiked beverages to the two-wheeled cowboys, to selling pieces of his southwestern furniture, including a carved eagle's head and rare Navaho rug, straight from the floor of his living room. Nothing was sacred, and there was no bridling the energy that accompanied the arrival of new money in town.

"Better get dressed and get on the bikes, we've got our first signing in an hour, at the Armory," the Colonel advised, interrupting a deal, between myself and Vic, for a turquoise necklace, currently on display around his wife's neck. I was never certain if she knew it was for sale.

Forty minutes later, and decked out in my increasingly ragged Ralph Lauren vintage cutoff denim and riding, helmet free, beside the feathered gas tank of the Colonel's Hog, I pulled off Route 90 at the first Sturgis exit and took my place in a backup of motorcycles that ran along a road bordered by huge tents, beneath which vendors were selling everything from jeans to jockey shorts (decorated, naturally, with the Harley logo), marquees advertising motorcycles of all kinds, parts and accessories, soft drinks and fast food stands, and people laid out in hammocks, either sleeping or still unconscious from last night's party. The air was a tantalizing blend of hot dogs, hamburgers, fried onions, motor oil, and gasoline.

As we inched closer to town, riding by storefronts that had, less than a week ago, been barber shops, dry cleaners, and other innocuous businesses, now converted to service depots for the varied needs of its new population, with everything from shops selling tempered steel fighting knives to Mike the Silver man and his sterling boot caps, I could hear the combined buzz of tattoo guns, like a swarm of angry bees.

Two hundred feet above our heads a blimp swayed gently in the wind, its logo a huge red "X" split by the words Excelsior-Henderson, one of the growing number of American bike manufacturers who intended to take a piece of the pie back from Harley-Davidson.

Founded by the Hanlon brothers of Minnesota, Excelsior had been jump-started by $15 million in private-equity capital before going public. In fact I had ridden one of their motorcycles at a book signing in Pike's Peak, Colorado. Mounted up and feeling a bit awkward on this big, new bike with its high saddle and huge exposed springs on the front end, I was just about to ride it from the lot, when one of their team, Dave, the man who had actually built it, waved me over and said quietly, "That bike you're sitting on is worth about $400,000. Enjoy the ride." It was Excelsior's prototype and his mention of its worth made me so uptight I could barely keep it balanced as I teetered out of the lot and did a very brief and careful circuit around the block.

I wondered how they were doing these days, in the sales department, since everything around me, except for the blimp, seemed to have Harley-Davidson stamped firmly on its tank—the other exception being a renegade in an "I Rode Mine" T-shirt, mounted proudly on an old, mud splattered Honda Dream.

We waited at a traffic light while a logjam of young, old, and in-betweens in jeans, T-shirts, and riding boots crossed like a tattooed centipede in front of us. I had never seen so many people crammed into one place in my life. The sidewalks were a quilt of bared and partially bared flesh, as Greg Allman sang "come on, let me show you my tattoo," from two lamppost-mounted speakers above our heads.

The Colonel signaled for a left turn after the light and we were on Main Street, which to either side and down the middle (leaving a single lane of one-way traffic up, and another down the opposite side), was a parking lot of iron and steel. Thousands of bikes, and thousands more people, in every conceivable shape, size, and state of dress and undress.

Where was my cabin companion from the airplane with her stick-on tattoos?

Suddenly, my wannabe best-selling book and my much prized masterpiece in chrome and borrowed money felt the first cruel rushes of dwarfism.

This was culture shock, with a blast of nitrous oxide on the side.

We were lucky to find a slip of pavement and the elbow room required to park and dismount. Then it was a full immersion into an ocean of shuffling, sweating, boozed up humanity, with the hint of marijuana wafting like pagan incense in the air around us.

Minutes later we surfaced on the stone steps of the Armory, a massive building with big doors and more people, spilling from them like refugees from a sinking boat.

"We're gonna sell some books," the Colonel repeated. I think it had become his mantra during the last crush of armpits and shoulders. "Keep going, inside and to the right."

Inside looked like Bingo night at the church bazaar. The walls were lined by booths and vendors, hustling the crowd and hawking wares which tended toward affordable items such as bumper stickers reading, "No Bar Too Far," and the much sought after "I Rode Mine" T-shirt.

Where was our banner, our tent, our pyramid of books, our dignity? Somehow, this was not the way I'd imagined it was going to be.

"Where are we set up?" I asked, eyeballing a stall which featured a pink candle that looked remarkably like a large phallus, ingeniously using the waxed scrotum as its base.

"With the tourist bureau," the Colonel answered.

"What?"

"Didn't want to invest in a stall, so I've made a few side deals."

"What kind of side deals?"

"Sort of like guest appearances," the Colonel explained, guiding me toward the far wall, beneath the sign for "Toilet," and in the direction of a large map of South Dakota.

"We'll spend a couple of hours at each stand, donate a few books to say thanks for the space, sell the rest and move on to the next. That way we cover the whole scene."

Made sense, in a Colonel kind of way. He had been working on the principle of creating reality by the force of mind—sort of the power of positive thinking with cosmic overtones—and had, many times, informed me that my book was already a best-seller, somewhere in the multilayered universe. Which layer, he wasn't quite sure of.

"Okay, let's do it," I said.

Marching forward to the three women behind the counter at the tourist board, we introduced ourselves.

Six hours and a handful of books lighter, including several charitable donations, we were still at it, but this time a block south of the Armory, sitting in twin card chairs, behind a wooden barrier and directly in front of a shirtless man, decorated from navel to chin in inked serpents, dragons and an inferno of orange flames and R.I.P. inscriptions, watching as he wielded his electric needle, clasped between the thick fingers of his surgically gloved hand, while creating a similar fresco on the bare back of a lady whose white breasts spilled generously from the sides of his operating table.

It must have been a hundred and ten degrees in the improvised tattoo studio and the only fan, of the cooling variety, was aimed at Dave the Rave's single client.

The Colonel and I might as well have been in a sauna.

"Do you really think we're going to draw a crowd in here?" I asked between bursts from the gun, when the needle was being dipped into another pot of blue pigment.

A moist ash fell like a single bead of sweat from the Colonel's Camel, mixing with the dust and butts already on the concrete floor.

"Be patient," he advised, although I thought he looked marginally more worried than he had at the airport.

Sturgis was going to be a tough nut to crack.

DOWN IN FLAMES

A BEAM OF SUNLIGHT slips through the crack in my closed eyelids and I jolt upright.

What time is it? I feel like I've been out for hours, but checking my watch I discover that I have been asleep for a grand total of ten minutes. Adequate time to completely disorient me.

I roll over and push myself up to my hands and knees then get to my feet. A couple of yoga-style maneuvers, including an agonizing effort to touch my toes, and the blood in my wounded knee is circulating enough to make walking a possibility.

Down the path and into the parking lot, intent on doing what I came here to do, which is to retrieve my Power Bar from my saddlebags, buy a can of iced tea from a vending machine and sit down on a picnic bench, and contemplate why every day in the saddle feels like a small lifetime.

But everything has changed.

There are a dozen bikes parked at the side of the detached trailer and a crowd of men milling round them, tightening saddle bags, sipping from cans of beer and

coke, and talking amongst themselves. One of them
laughs. It's a big, gruff laugh that cuts straight through
me. Then I notice.

The Big Dog is gone.

In its place, glistening beneath the bright sun, is a low,
fat bike with a wide back tire. The black gasoline tank is
flamed and the flames, brilliant red, give it a sinister, outlaw look.

My stomach feels like it has suddenly dropped from my
body and hit the ground, leaving a sick hollow.

I walk faster, toward the men. Where's the Big Dog? It's
got to be here. Got to be.

I stop about twenty feet from the black and red bike.

I didn't lock it. I'd thought about it but there was nobody around and I was too tired. Too lazy. Too sloppy.
Now I've lost a thirty thousand dollar motorcycle that I
don't own.

I rein in my panic and try for a rational explanation.
Maybe I left it someplace else. I've done it with cars, in
big parking lots.

It's still here, somewhere, I tell myself.

I walk faster. Away from the bikes and the men and
along the concrete sidewalk, past the circular building
with the maps, past the public pay phones, all the time
combing the parking lot with my eyes, searching.

Walking past a few picnic tables, the soft drinks machine, a couple of cars, a few kids playing ball on the grass.
To the far end of the lot. Still, no Big Dog.

This is bad, very bad.

I try to stay calm, to go over things, retracing my route
into the lot. I remember the trailer. I remember leaving
the bike by the trailer. Wondering what it was doing there,
detached and vacant. Then the idea hits me. The trailer
could be some kind of lookout. It begins to make sense.

A few hundred miles from Sturgis, people pushing themselves, trying to ride the last leg of their journey, tired and spent, forgetting to lock their bikes. Disappearing into the welcome station, or up the mountain trail while the lookout inside the trailer phones the boys. "We've got one."

The bad guys ride in like everybody else, and park-up, close to the targeted bike, probably forming a circle around so it's not obvious when the mechanic hot-wires the ignition and rides it away. All done in about thirty seconds.

The Big Dog is probably en route to a chop shop.

What do I do? Call Nick Messer and tell him that the bike's been stolen, that I didn't lock it, that I didn't even shut off the petcock? That I'm an asshole? I can't even manage that. I don't have my phone, or Messer's cell number for that matter. They were in the saddlebags. Everything—my phone, my clothes, my toothbrush, my diary—is inside the saddlebags.

I feel absolutely useless.

I decide to call the police.

I turn and begin to walk toward the pay phones. But I can't call the law. The bike doesn't have a legal license plate. I don't know the vehicle identification number. I don't have a U.S. bike license. All in all, I'm only a couple of notches more legal than whoever stole it.

Everything is collapsing inside me. I feel my throat constrict as I psychologically teeter on the brink of a meltdown.

Then, a heartbeat before I sink beneath the mire of every past bad deed and insecurity in my life, comes a rush of resolve. I turn and stare at the detached trailer with the curtained windows. Maybe all is not lost.

Maybe the lookout is still inside the trailer.

Maybe I can get the bike back.

I walk to the back and listen through the door. There's nothing from inside, not a sound. All I can hear are the voices from the men who are still standing around their bikes.

There are five of them. They don't look particularly evil, in fact they don't look anywhere near as evil as I do, with my long, filthy matted hair, my beet-red nose, stubble of beard and chipmunk eyes, like tight white circles against a wind burnt backdrop, matching the lens of my dark glasses.

I walk up to the biggest of them.

"How long you been here?"

Taken by surprise, the man steps back, unsure where I have come from, what I want, and whether I'm talking to him. I see what I interpret as a spark of fear in his eyes—a sure sign of guilt.

"How long?" I repeat, attempting to control a developing quaver in my voice.

His hands rise instinctively, palms open, as he expects to be assaulted, probably by my inflamed nose, and hasn't got a clue why.

"Ten minutes, maybe," he answers.

Another voice catches me from the side. "Why? What's going on?"

I keep my eyes on the big man while answering, "Somebody stole my motorcycle. Maybe you guys saw what happened."

"We didn't see anything," the big man says.

I'm not buying that.

"It was a black bike, with purple flames on the tank."

There is a long silence, before the man in front of me answers.

"It wasn't here when we pulled in. I'm pretty sure of that."

"It's a Big Dog," I continue, feeling even more sick inside as I begin to realize that these guys are probably not part of some outlaw conspiracy and have nothing to do with my missing bike.

"A what?"

"A Big Dog."

"There was nothing here but that red and black bike in back of you," he says.

I turn and look at the black bike with the red flames.

Everything seems to click into a fresh visual perspective. I see clear white letters, glaring at me like a billboard, bursting from the red flames on the gas tank.

They spell Big Dog. It seems impossible, but it's true.

"That's my bike!"

My laugh, a mixture of relief and nerves, sounds like a yelp, as if someone has just sneaked up behind me and bit me on the ass.

No one joins in. Instead everyone, all five of them, turn and stare at the Big Dog.

"But it didn't look like that when I left it. It was different. Damn thing's changed color."

I walk toward the bike and the color of the flames mutate from red to orange, then back to red as I change direction and look at it from the rear. From the top, looking down, as I usually do when I ride, the color is a deep purple.

"Look at it," I say. "It changes every time you move."

Now, all of us are walking around the bike, marveling at the shifting colors, red to orange and back again. The tank seems alive in the shimmering sunlight.

"Must be some kind of special paint," someone suggests, as vaguely I remember Nick Messer mentioning that the bike had a harlequin finish. Not knowing what he'd meant, I'd paid no particular attention to him.

"Yeah, must be," I agree, looking down at the see-through dash as if I need final confirmation that it is, in fact, the Big Dog, the same bike I rode in on.

Then I turn to the others, feeling that I owe them an explanation for my erratic behavior.

"You see, it's not my bike. Not exactly. What I mean is I'm riding it for the company that makes them and I've never noticed that it changed colors, not till now, and I thought you guys—well—anyway—" I realize from their dumbfounded expressions that it's definitely time to retire from the road and lock myself up in a hotel room, for everyone's sake.

"You going to Sturgis?" I ask, getting on the motorcycle.

"Yeah."

Another few seconds of silence.

Finally, borrowing the ancient mariner's line from underneath the bridge, I say, "See you up the road."

Feeling their eyes on my back as I ride slowly from the lot, replaying the whole episode in my head with varying outcomes. But what if—?

MRS. P'S

WHAT IF. THERE'S ALWAYS A WHAT IF —what if I had never made the telephone call to the South American lady?

I had been married nearly eighteen years and out of the dating game for nearly twenty, which was almost the age gap between us. I was, potentially, on the verge of making a fool of myself, but I felt compelled, particularly after a saki soaked evening in the Kyoto tub. At Albany, with no television, no radio, and a record player that had last hosted Dean Martin singing "Volare" on it's 33 r.p.m. turntable, my life had become monastic.

Country rides on the Springer, visits to Warrs, the boxing club in Bermondsey, and conversations with my dying friend Josef—the only person I knew who still considered me, at fifty, a young man with a great future—were my only real contacts with the outside world.

And, despite of my vows of chastity (till the divorce matter was settled) to lawyer Raymond Tooth, there was the element of lust. That was undeniable. There was just something about the way her jeans fit the contours of the saddle of her Sportster that sparked my fantasies. The fact that she was romantically involved with a young actor and employed by my estranged wife added the element of forbidden fruit to the mix.

Basically, I was out of my mind.

So I made the call, braced by several cups of saki, froze a moment when I heard her voice, then suggested a bike ride the upcoming weekend.

To my amazement she agreed, with the stipulation that we were back in London by evening so that she could attend a party with her boyfriend, making it clear to me that this was an act of friendship. I assured her that would be no problem as I had a pressing engagement myself— in the bathtub with a liter of saki (although I kept that detail to myself)—and agreed on a meeting place on the outskirts of town.

A day in the saddle, or a day following hers—it was a lot to imagine for an incarcerated man. Sleep on the tatami was sweaty with anticipation.

Finally, bike and boots spit shined, the morning came.

The A3 was one of my favorite roads during my past life. It intersected with Kingston Hill, making it just a roll downward from the garage of the manor house. It felt strange passing by, almost as if I should be turning off and riding up, knocking on the old wood door and shouting, "I'm home!" Probably to find the alleged voodoo doll floating in the sensory deprivation tank with a pin through its heart. It felt sad anyway, knowing that for many reasons, I could never go back and that my ex-wife and I would probably never be friends again.

Particularly after the ride I was about to take.

We met at a place where the A3, the main highway, intersected with a smaller road which led south, to the coast and followed along the sea.

She was wearing black leather pants, a black leather jacket, a black helmet, and riding goggles reminiscent of a W.W. II fighter pilot. In the context of her face, which was long and chiseled with shining brown eyes, a beautifully defined jaw, fine, full lips, and silken smooth skin, her nose, on the large side, sat perfectly, giving her a look that I attributed to Spanish aristocracy. On that day beneath her helmet and accentuated by the goggles, all I could see was a nose, which came as a relief. I figured if I concentrated on that I could keep my thoughts on the road, particularly if I stayed either to her side or in front of her on the bike, avoiding the tail section.

It worked.

We rode for miles, away from town and, for me, away from the snowballing ugliness that had become my divorce, with friends choosing sides, the British tabloid press running absurd stories, possibly fueled by my old friend, La Plante Production's one woman P.R. team, and the lawyers digging in their heels.

I just wanted out.

It occurred to me, while we rode the flat, two-lane highway south, that the thing that I craved most was this woman's respect. She had known me before the war had begun, and she was still hearing the office dirt, but she was on the road with me, and that meant everything.

The ride was therapy, and sometime later, over lunch at a small pub, with a glass of whiskey in my hand I asked her why she had accepted my offer.

"Because we're friends," she answered simply.

It was exactly what I needed. Many who had claimed undying loyalty had gone with the money and would no longer speak to me, afraid of losing their positions within the power structure. I recall one such man—out jogging with his dogs—seeing me in the street, then doing a complete about-face and sprinting in the opposite direction.

After lunch we rode on, relaxed by the alcohol, along the rocky coastline with the slate gray Atlantic to our left, as the clouds began to gather above our heads. It was about four o'clock in the afternoon and we were about to turn around and head back to London when the Springer began to buck, as if it was being starved for gas. I threw the petcock to reserve and continued to ride but something was definitely wrong. The bike seemed to be choking.

There was a sign for a village and a turn off the main road which we followed down into a hamlet which seemed little more than a short row of houses and an eighteenth century pub, like a small stone fortress.

We rode into the parking lot of the pub and got off the bikes.

The first thing I did was check the gas in the tank, which was three quarters full, after which I turned the petcock back to the on position and revved the motorcycle, hoping that whatever was clogging it would work its way through the carburetor. Everything seemed fine, so we got back on the bikes and took off, only to have the Springer sputter and die at the first hill, on the way out of the hamlet. Turning around, I rolled the bike back into the lot and shut it off.

"It's never done this before," I said, twisting the throttle and hitting the starter button for the fifth time as the battery ebbed and the starter motor clicked.

"Maybe you're flooding it," my riding companion suggested.

Her explanation seemed good enough, along with the light sprinkle of rain, to warrant a move to the inner regions of the pub adjacent to the parking lot.

There is nothing like an English country pub on a wet

afternoon. After a blustery day on the road, it was like
walking into a cocoon. Inside, beneath the low, white plas-
ter ceilings and thick wooden rafters, a fire was roaring,
warming the air and filling it with the scent of burning
wood. The locals, all six of them, were friendly and talk-
ative, mainly about the big rain that was supposed to
sweep in by nightfall.

Rain, how many inches?

I panicked.

How were we going to get back to London? Picturing a
tabloid picture of myself, arms wrapped round my estranged wife's script editor, riding the back of her Sportster into the center of town, the picture then landing on
the desk of La Plante Productions, to be faxed immediately to Ray Tooth's office, as he choked on his morning
cigar.

I had another shot of whiskey to settle my nerves.

"Better try the bike again," I said.

Outside, the rain was falling harder and it was getting
dark, and cold.

The Springer was dead.

"Maybe I should call the A.A."

Back into the pub, onto the pay phone, to be informed
that there would be up to a two hour wait. Time for another whiskey, or two.

An hour passed with no sign of rescue, and finally,
guilty for keeping her from London and her social life, and
concerned that we might be discovered together, I suggested she take off for home, without me.

Outside again, this time for the farewell, and the rain
was belting the bikes with real vengeance, night was falling
and the sky was low and ugly. We were both mildly drunk,
or maybe more.

"I don't think you should ride right now," I said, both

concerned for her and selfish for another piece of her time. "Let's go back inside and have something to eat."

"That sounds good," she replied. Seemingly a lot less concerned about the situation than I was.

By now, our frequent in and out appearances at the pub were being greeted by the locals, including a large sheep-dog with a gift for flatulence, with all the enthusiasm of a continuing soap opera. Were we leaving? Were we staying? Would the motor start? Had the rain hit yet? Did we want another drink, just to warm up?

We were just short of a round of applause by our third reentrance.

After two plates of shepherd's pie at the bar, and a couple more single malts, someone suggested we try the hamlet's one and only bed and breakfast, Mrs. P's, less than ten meters from the door of the pub.

I looked at my companion, with her honest brown eyes, long dark hair swirling halfway down her back and leather pants tight to her long thighs and tried to rekindle memories of her face beneath the black helmet, and her eyes behind the aviator goggles. Concentrate on her nose, I told myself. The truth was, nose and all, she looked good to me, the best thing I'd seen in a very long time.

Spend the night together?

I'd do it, but would she?

"What do you think?" I asked.

"I could lose my job, but it does sound better than eighty miles in the rain," she replied.

A cancellation call to the boyfriend, one to the A.A., and a couple of locks on the bikes and by nine o'clock we were wading throughout the downpour to the cottage of Mrs. P, which, as promised, was only a wobble and weave from the door of the pub.

She answered our knock in a pink bathrobe, looking like

a silver-haired Margaret Thatcher, carrying a flashlight, which she used to examine us both thoroughly before explaining that her best room had already been taken, leaving only a small single on the downstairs floor, which shared a toilet and shower with the guests next door. We could have it, along with two clean towels, a bar of soap and breakfast, for seventeen pounds and fifty pence ($30.00).

I registered us under the name of Mr. and Mrs. Herbie Rainwater, the name of a guy I had once known in high school. It was the first name that came into my head when confronted with the guest registry, and we were shown to our accommodations, which were, as promised, small, with a single bed pressed against a wall so thin that the conversation of the next-door guests, a man and woman, discussing the price of a liter of petrol in Cornwall as compared to the same on the south coast, came through like a radio broadcast.

Mrs. P bid us good-night, leaving us with the promised twin towels, a bar of soap and strict instructions that breakfast would be served in the dining room between six and nine.

The door was closed and we were alone with the sound of rain pelting the windows.

What was proper etiquette? Should I sleep in my helmet, full leathers, and boots, or risk rejection by stripping down to my undershorts and socks?

My friend answered with a quick flick of the light switch. In the darkness I could hear her boots and sopping wet leathers hitting the floor, the same floor that hosted my hopeful, but exhausted, body a few minutes later.

The following morning, directly after a bowl of damp cornflakes, a slice of buttery toast, and braced by a cup of proper English breakfast tea, with the sun shining and the air clear, the Springer started with the first press of the button, and rode like a dream, all the way back to London.

Fate had knocked, the Springer had answered.

There are no what ifs.

Only what is.

TRANSPARENT

BY FIVE O'CLOCK IN THE AFTERNOON I'm virtually, in sailing terms, hiking out over the side of the motorcycle. The reason for this extreme lean angle is the wind whistling across the plains. Howling is more like it, treating my body like a sail, and forcing me to compensate by leaning into it for counterbalance. It feels like I'm sliding sideways down the highway.

This trip has been like a thrill ride in an amusement park, just when it seems to have peaked, there's another surprise. Four days ago, or whenever it was that the Big Dog and I rolled out of the Hamptons, I would have had a hard time handling this stuff, but now, veteran of floods, bin-lined boots, steak teriyaki, and imagined bike theft, I am able to accept my tilted circumstances and ride on, along with the multitude of two-wheeled side winders behind and ahead of me, all hell bent on the Promised Land.

What is the draw of this small town up the road? Why does the word Sturgis hold such magnetism for the American biker?

Maybe it's the cowboy in us, the freedom of riding bare headed along the old roads between Sturgis and Custer, swooping down into the cool of the canyons and flying up the sunny sides of the mountains, breaking for the hairpin turns and cruising through tunnels cut through solid granite and out into the Badlands with their summits of jagged rock and desolate expanses of eroded earth, with no thought of anything but the road and the ride, and the prospect of making town and hitching the bike to a post and getting something cold to drink at one of the bars and saloons that line the dusty sidewalks.

Part of it has to be the shared consciousness of the motorcycle itself, particularly the American motorcycle, this rumbling, fuel guzzling dinosaur among the high-tech road rockets of Japan, or the quiet, reliable, and efficient machines of Germany. The fact is nothing else sounds or rides like an American bike. You either love it or hate it, and everyone at Sturgis loves it. That's the common thread.

The Colonel and I spent ten days in Sturgis, and during that time I felt myself change. It took a few days and a few more "appearances," but eventually we were both wrapped into the rhythm of the place. Assimilated. The Armory and its battery of vendors became a morning stop, with familiar faces and shared quips on the customers and sales, while lunch was a ten mile ride to Spearfish and a shady seat in the Quadalajara, devouring tacos and that staple of all Mexican cuisine, the Margarita.

The red Big Dog trailer was a pit stop on the way back into town. Mohawk was usually stationed in the rear, door open, gate down, doing on the spot road repairs, while Nick and Sheldon worked the walk-by traffic out in front, where the show bikes were on display. Behind them, on Lazalle Street, the parade of pumped up machines and bodies continued all day and into the night. It was there, in that parking lot behind the civic center that I first thought of the simple silver bike, and there that I figured out how to pay for it, with a trade-in—following a consultation with Mohawk—using the Highway Cruiser. The deal was consummated by an evening with the entire Big Dog crew, myself, and the Colonel, at the Quadalajara.

I recall riding home that night, relaxed and happy, as if life had been made complete by the silver bike and the fact that my friends were going to build it for me. Josef's words were clear in my head, "Relationships are all that counts, the rest is bullshit."

The Silver Bike was clean, like a new beginning.

We met Big Jim and Nancy later that afternoon at the Armory, and Gary, a gentle soul with Atlas shoulders who had read every book I'd ever written.

Sturgis was beginning to feel like family, a way of life, far removed from the hustle and competition of New York.

At a press conference, Senator Ben Nighthorse Campbell from Colorado, decked out in leather cutoffs with his Native American insignia on the back, spoke of his reason for being in Sturgis, to see the unspoiled country and have the chance to ride through the Black Hills, a sacred site to the Native Americans of the region. Sturgis was about respect, for other people and their way of life, and for the land itself. Perhaps that's the reason that with so many gathered, there were so few acts of violence.

In many ways Sturgis was like entering a different society, with a different set of values and customs. I met heart surgeons and pawn brokers, grandmas and preachers, but without the façade of money and status, my interaction was at personal level, with no ulterior motives.

The talk was of the weather, the best rides, and the most interesting bikes.

I'm not going to make it tonight. The wind is blowing, the sun is melting my nose, I'm tired and the bike needs gas. On top of that I've lost my desperation. I've finally out ridden my deadlines. All I want is that quiet room and a hard bed.

The next exit is Murdo, about a hundred and fifty miles from Sturgis, which will give me time to get clean and rested, then ride in first thing in the morning.

I'm not the only one with this idea. As I pull off Route 90 and ride down the main street of town, turning left into the parking lot of the Best Western, I see, by the number of other bikes already in residence, that I've got a lot of company.

Still, I get a room, chain the bike to a post, draw the blinds, turn on the air conditioner, and lay back on the bed. Beyond the walls, the roar of westbound motorcycles is a continuous and strangely relaxing drone. It occurs to me that I don't actually know what day it is, and I have a hard time figuring out how many days I've been traveling. Time on the road is measured more by the sequence of events than chronology, and the events that stand out in my mind have begun to run together, without a clear divide.

There is great value in spending this type of time alone. It provides a chance to reorder my thoughts, and rediscover my basic values. I miss my wife and son, but I feel they will be getting a more complete person at the end of our time apart, because I will be more at peace with myself.

The saddle of a motorcycle is a great place, as Sandy

said—way back on the fairgrounds of Indiana—to "think things through."

Sometimes, after a day on the bike, particularly a day in which I've had a slip in concentration, a skid, or a near miss, I have contemplated my own death, wondered what the transition from life to whatever lies beyond will be like and if I will be ready to make it. I think of John, forty-three years old, with his four young daughters and his beloved Harley in the garage below his bedroom. He left me a reminder of himself, his Department of Corrections badge. It is a shiny metal shield, attached to an oval shaped patch of black leather. I keep it in my desk drawer and sometimes, when I'm feeling down and indulgent, with feelings of lethargy or depression, I take it out and hold it in my hand, rubbing my thumb over the blue and white enamel emblem in the center, with the silver eagle, wings spread, sitting above it, thinking of the many times John clipped this same badge to his belt and headed off to work with his delinquent boys. That was his job, part of his life. Till one day it was over, ready or not.

I think of Josef, learning his final lessons, about the ultimate futility of power, money and ego, and the importance of personal relationships, in the sanctity of his tiny flat, with his emotions so close to the surface that he would often cry as we spoke.

Or my dad, waiting for me at the funeral home, on the gurney in his white gown, teaching me that all flesh, even my own, is destined for dust.

Yet, on the bike, riding at eighty with the wind in my face, the sound of the engine, twin cylinders beating strong and steady, and the big sky above, I am without age or constraint of any kind, in a place without the gravity of a past or future, given only to the moment, a hair's breadth from sudden death, yet totally alive.

Five o'clock in the afternoon and, outside, it's hot, a hundred and three degrees if the thermometer on the side of the office building is accurate. There are bikes tethered to railings all along the line of rooms. A few have been covered with tarpaulins, and a few more are sitting in trailers, shined and ready to tow, or to roll down for the final leg of the ride into Sturgis.

There is a swimming pool on the street side of the parking lot. The water is exploding with reflected bursts of sunlight, and there is not another person in the lot. I figure with this heat, most of them are behind the doors and curtains of their rooms with the air conditioners on at full blast. I don't have a bathing suit but I am wearing a reasonably clean set of white Calvin Klein boxers.

I walk into the fenced enclosure and take a quick look around. There are a few cars and bikes passing along the main street in front of the hotel but no people on foot, so it's out of my boots, jeans and shirt and into the pool in my Calvin Kleins. Swimming down, until my face is hovering just above the bottom at the deep end. I remain there, holding my breath in suspended animation, where the world is cool and silent.

In the East End of Long Island, surrounded by everything that money can buy, where most backyards have a swimming pool and many have a private ocean or bay beach, access to water is taken for granted.

But here, in the blacktopped parking lot of the Great Western motel, somewhere in the middle of South Dakota, with the sun blistering the pavement till it's impossible to stand barefoot in one place for more than a few seconds, this twelve-by-twenty-four-foot concrete shell, filled with water, is priceless.

I surface from my bliss to find a man and woman, clad

in proper swimming attire, flip flops on their feet and towels in hand, heading from a corner room, in the direction of the enclosure.

I smile and say hello as they enter, watching as they sidestep my boots and make their way to two lounge chairs, which are positioned almost directly in front of the ladder. They are an older, very civilized looking couple. He has neatly trimmed gray hair and a John Grisham novel with him and she has her hair wrapped in what looks like a turban to conceal the curlers beneath. I can't imagine them riding any of the motorcycles that surround the courtyard, and doubt seriously if they've ever spent a night at the Rath.

"Hot one, huh?" I comment as I make my way up the ladder, having had my turn in the water.

"Yes, very," she answers, smiling.

I'm on the third rung when I happen to look down. Discovering to my shock that, wet, my Calvin Kleins are completely transparent.

Whoa! As I slip back into the water.

She doesn't bat an eye, and he settles into the lounge chair and opens his book.

I reckon I got away with it, but how the hell do I get out of the pool? No matter which route I take, including plans for a heroic double arm exit from the deep end, like the upward motion of a dip on parallel bars, I've still got to walk in front of them to gather my boots and clothing.

Luckily, after a few minutes treading water, and trying to appear as if I'm involved in some form of Navy SEAL inspired aquatic exercise routine, they decide to take a swim. As soon as they're in, I'm headed out, darting past them like a moray eel, up the ladder, no doubt treating them to a full screen view of my saddle-sore posterior, rosy from the long exposure to the water, as I bend to grab my belongings before hotfooting it across the lot to my room.

TATTOO

LATER, IN DRY KLEINS AND AT DINNER, I am seated alone in a wooden booth at the far end of a restaurant-bar which is a few blocks down the street from the Great Western. It's still early, six o'clock, the place is nearly deserted, and I am confronting a rib-eye steak, green salad, and a bottle of Corona when I hear the rumble of bikes through the wall. Blub-Blub-Blub-Blub. Then silence. A minute later two men walk in, dressed in T-shirts and jeans, giving the place the once-over before walking past me on their way to a booth in the back. Meeting my eyes and nodding a greeting. They appear friendly enough, but there is that moment of hesitation, as if they may know me, and my instincts are aroused.

A few minutes later, one of them gets up from the booth and walks past, glancing quickly at me again, then out the door.

At least this time I've locked the bike.

He's back a few seconds later, walking past with another furtive glance before heading in the direction of his friend.

I'm draining the last of the Corona and wondering what

they're up to when both of them arrive at my table.

I look up.

The spokesman has a square, friendly face, with the chipmunk eyes that I associate with long days in the saddle.

"Pardon me," he says.

"Yes?"

"We thought we recognized your tattoo," he continues.

"My tattoo?"

"The one on your forearm."

I look down at my forearm. The tattoo he's referring to is a Celtic bird, done in greeny-blue. It sits about four inches below my elbow and wraps all the way around my forearm, like a band, with the elongated neck and head on the top side of my arm while the legs and talons are on the underside. The tattoo is about ten years old, and was put on by Ian of Reading, in his studio, about thirty miles south of London. An indelible piece of my past life, I've had it long enough that I'm no longer conscious of it being there. It's part of me.

"You wrote about that tattoo in your book, didn't you?"

I cock my head and smile. Is this guy talking about *Hog Fever*? Was he a buyer of one of that lucky two hundred the Colonel and I unloaded when last in Sturgis?

"That's why I went outside to check your bike, to see if it was the same one you had in the book," he continues. "The one that cost you all that money."

Oh, yeah, there's no mistake about it. Suddenly I feel like I'm looking into the faces of two old friends, and, after confirming that they've got the right tattoo, I tell them all about the floods of Iowa, the Big Dog and the wonders of reliable travel.

"But where is that other bike, the one from the book, the Springer?"

It's a strange question. Sort of like he's asking me about

an old and particularly difficult love affair, something I've not quite gotten over. It brings back memories, many of them broken down by the side of the road, and all of them costly.

"The Springer should be in Sturgis right now," I reply.

With Big Jim in the saddle.

The Springer has been in his keeping since the Colonel retired as the official voice of midlife biking.

It all started at the Armory, in Sturgis—during our stint with the tourist bureau—when flanked by Gary and Nancy, Jim asked the Colonel if we would be available for a book signing in Dallas, at Christmas. The Colonel checked our calendar; it was thin for the fall. No problem, we were available.

I arrived by plane from New York, and the Colonel hauled the bikes and the books in the Fargo trailer from Indianapolis, a distance of about nine hundred miles. Unfortunately his load, figuring that each book weighed about a pound and we had sold only about two hundred at Sturgis, was not much lighter than it had been for his journey to South Dakota, so the fifty mile an hour speed limit was observed. He was tired, and it took a few drinks to lift his mustache.

Big Jim is a scuba diving instructor with an underwater business in Cozumel, but I believe he missed his true calling as an evangelical minister (although he has since been ordained and is, according to him, the toast of the Dallas wedding circuit). He's Jimmy Swaggart in ostrich skin boots, custom-made, with a clear and resonant voice that belongs in a pulpit. Give Jim a crowd and a microphone and prepare to be converted to whatever he's selling.

The Colonel and I watched in awe as he MCed the HOG bash in Dallas, raffling away Christmas gifts with the ease of a TV host on a shopping network before dispensing with complimentary copies of my book—I seemed destined to be a giveaway, but after all it was Christmas—then grabbing Nancy for a quick Texas two-step across the floor of the Holiday Inn, to the tunes of the Beach Boys.

The Colonel and I were installed on Nancy's twin sofas, I was placed in charge of all mixed drinks while Jim organized a signing at the local Harley dealership and another at Easyriders of Dallas, owned by Rick Fairless—who by incredible coincidence had bought my Battistini stretch from Big Dog.

With both my old bikes in Dallas I felt right at home. The weekend went smoothly, and after the festivities, the Colonel's intention was to stay on the road between Dallas and Indianapolis long enough to establish a network of bike dealers who would distribute the book, a feat no book company was willing to attempt because bike dealers were outside the computerized network of book dealers and there would be no reliable way of collecting payments.

By now it was winter, the Colonel's corporate office was being warmed with a blow heater, and all attempts at making the book an official Harley accessory had been met with a stony silence on the part of our would-be mentors in Milwaukee. Leaving the Colonel alone on the road, searching for that one place in the universe where the book was a best-seller and being met by lots of grease stained fingers, thumbing the pages, accompanied by a gruff voice, saying, "Don't sell nothin' but trade manuals out of this shop."

There were exceptions. One was Motorcycles of Indianapolis, with Scott Rattermann at the helm. A friend of the Colonel's, he embraced both the book and myself as a brother in arms, or chains, and hosted a couple of spectacular gatherings at his showroom, with people riding two hundred miles to shake hands, get a book and talk about motorcycles. If there had been a few more like Scott, with both vision and organizational talent, the Colonel and I could have gone public.

As it was, after Dallas, with nine hundred miles of snow and icy highway, anonymous hotels, and unannounced drop-ins on some of the dreariest souls this side of motorized travel, the Colonel was suffering a long, slow death by refrigeration. By the time Indianapolis came into sight, he was tugging on the ends of his mustache and praying for divine intervention.

Which came in the form of Big Jim, who, from somewhere deep in the cosmos, must have heard the call—Mayday.

"I think I could move a lot of books down here," he announced by telephone. "And I sure would like to have that Springer."

Funded by a man, who for reasons of privacy—the main one being that his wife had no idea he was bankrolling a fledgling book empire—remained in the shadows, four thousand copies of *Hog Fever* arrived at Nancy's house in Dallas. Little did she know that she had just become the new corporate landlord. They padded her living room floor and lined the walls of her guest bedroom. They were stacked six feet high. They took over.

"Now, let's talk about that Springer." Big Jim was relentless. "Can't sell the books without the bike." I heard the line before, and knew where it led.

I was in need of cash. I was about to build a house, was in process of building the Silver Bike and had no place to store a razor blade, let alone the Springer. We settled on sixteen thousand dollars—about the value of the chrome—on one condition, that I could buy it back when I had the money. By then I wanted to use it as the centerpiece in our new living room, although I hadn't run the idea past my wife.

The Colonel was out of the book business, although he promised to remain available in an advisory capacity. Getting away with his shirt, in fact several hundred shirts, T-shirts to be exact, all emblazoned with a circular red sign reading *Hog Fever*, No Cure.

The last time I saw Big Jim he was wearing jeans, a "Divers Do It Underwater" T-shirt and his custom-made ostrich skins, standing with a microphone in his hand, in the center of two hundred intoxicated cowboys at Stroker's Ice House, which sits adjacent to the Easyriders dealership, on the west side of Dallas.

Bellowing. "You fellas want to see what a guy from East Hampton looks like?!"

The response was less than enthusiastic.

"Well, do ya?!"

It was a hundred and six degrees on the road and nobody gave a shit about a guy from East Hampton, let alone knew where it was.

"Come on, put your hands together!"

I believe I heard someone clap, but it may as easily have been a belch from the other end of the bar.

"I can't hear ya!?"

At the time that this mania was taking place I was seated on a stool at the back of the room, sipping a Tequiza, a pre-mix in a bottle that tasted like beer with a splash of tequila and a drop of lime juice added, trying to look as if I had nothing to do with what was taking place center stage, and praying for that first hint of inebriation that would dull my embarrassment.

"Now is that any way to treat a bro from East Hampton?!" Big Jim continued, upping his considerable vocal heft by an octave.

I sank lower down on the stool and sucked hard on the Tequiza.

"Let's give'm a warm Texas welcome!"

Still nothing.

"He's written a book called *Hog Fever*. You want a laugh, you ought read it . . . C'mon!" Resorting to the Colonel's old tactics.

The continuing silence was punctuated by the hiss of someone opening a can of beer.

"Hell, maybe you guys can't read!"

I eyed the nearest exit.

"Damn it," he shouted. "I still can't hear ya!"

And lo and behold, finally inspired by that pure voice of God, it came. A single clap at first, followed by another, then another, a couple of whistles and there was Big Jim, nodding his head and smiling beatifically, as he motioned me to come forward and repent.

I slinked to the microphone, hoping I wouldn't be required to give a small speech about the Harley scene in East Hampton, comprised mainly of cigar smoking tycoons with a weekend's stubble of beard, loud pipes, two hundred miles on the clock, Armani jackets, and skull cap helmets.

Fortunately, the great orator was unwilling to relinquish the mike, or the obvious spell he'd cast upon the crowd. Allowing me to skulk suspiciously in the background while he raffled off three free copies of my book.

"Hell, if ya can't sell em, give 'em away, at least it spreads the word," he whispered wisely while licking his rosy lips as we tramped through puddles of spilt beer on our way out into the Texas sunshine.

Later that evening, I was seated at Nancy's dining room table in Garland, a Dallas suburb, with Gary, armed with two razor sharp knives—one in his pocket, one in his boot—and a concealed Glock in his shoulder holster, passing me the books—one at a time—as I attempted to sign the remaining three thousand, nine hundred and ninety-seven copies—"They're worth more with a signature," Jim reasoned. Made sense, considering he'd been giving them away all day.

It was during one of my two-hour sessions at the signature table, squeezed between three columns of books and a mahogany casket, which Jim had acquired during a previous career as an undertaker, that I expressed interest in riding cross-country to Sturgis, and it was at that point that Nancy, an airline employee who always kept the traveler's comfort in mind, suggested I consider a rainsuit. Jim kindly volunteered hers, to save me any unnecessary expense, and I agreed to return it when we met in Sturgis.

"I'm taking the Springer," he promised. "And we'll have a few books for sale at the campground."

It was deja vu.

Big Jim, Nancy, Gary, Big Dog, the Springer, the Silver Bike, all waiting down the road.

But tonight, sitting in the saddle of the motorcycle, parked outside my room at the Great Western, with the stars spilled like a chest of rainbow-colored gems above my head, I don't feel the need to go anywhere at all.

I don't feel the need, for anything.

DAY SIX

WHEN THE WAY COMES TO AN END, THEN
CHANGE—HAVING CHANGED, YOU PASS
THROUGH.

—I CHING

LADY LUCK

THERE'S A GREAT SONG, written by Tom Waits and covered by the Eagles. I'm not certain of the title but a part of the lyric, "now the sun's coming up and I'm riding with Lady Luck" repeats over and over again in my mind as I ride from the slip road and onto Route 90.

It's six o'clock in the morning, the sky is pale blue and the sun is rising, reflected in my mirror. There are already a number of trucks and bikes on the road, and everyone is making time, heading west.

The Big Dog feels like home. I love this bike. Through the heat, the rain, and the floods, it's never quit.

Fifty miles from Sturgis, a stop for gas and breakfast, the wind picks up, and more bikes join the procession. I begin to feel the gravity of the place, pulling me towards it. This is what I've come for, I tell myself, Sturgis and the Silver Bike.

Past Spearfish, home of Trader Vic and last resting place for me and the Colonel, then down the home stretch, the road bordered by campgrounds and motels. Every sign reads "No Vacancy."

It's nine o'clock in the morning and there are already a lot of bikes on the road. Two wheels, three wheels, a rainbow of colored tanks, riders with long hair, short hair, no hair at all.

Here I come. Almost home. I rode mine, traveling with Lady Luck, all the way from New York, from the tip of the island.

The first exit for Sturgis comes into view and I have a nervous tickle in my belly, excitement building.

Signal right, slow down, from seventy to fifty, from fifty to thirty, from thirty to twenty, ten. Stop. There's already a minor traffic jam. Bikes are lined up all the way from the off-ramp to the traffic light, extending a good quarter mile up the road. The early morning sun is baking the macadam till it steams and the air is permeated by the scent of gasoline and motor oil. The sound of motorcycles is like one huge revving engine, becoming a kind of white noise.

I sit, revving with the rest of them, bathed in exhaust fumes. I've got this feeling. I can't quite define it but it's there, gnawing away at my gut.

I look to my left and backward, across the denim shoulder of the rider behind me and see Highway 90, heading west. Miles and miles of highway, like a winding ribbon of gray, extending all the way to the Pacific Coast. Miles and miles of riding. My body senses an inertia. It wants to keep moving, accustomed to the feeling of the bike beneath it and the wind in its face. Used to the freedom of the road.

The feeling becomes a yearning, and a sadness that the trip is over. I feel as if I have scaled the mountain only to find that I've been climbing backward and wound up at the bottom. The golden eagle above my head has been replaced by the Excelsior-Henderson blimp, a fat silver balloon, bobbing lazily in the currents of warm air.

The light changes and the bikes begin to move, a little at a time, with a throaty disjointed rhythm. Finally I'm rolling down the gentle rise, onto Route 79 and Junction Avenue. Past the first of the trader's stalls displaying their latest in shotgun exhaust pipes and gunfighter saddles, past a large stand with racks and racks of leather coats, riding chaps, and T-shirts.

The big, squared building that houses the National Motorcycle Museum is on my right, home of a 1907 Harley, the oldest unrestored, fully-functioning Harley-Davidson in existence. Steve McQueen's 1915 Cyclone is in there, too. Out in front dealers are opening the backs of long, deep trailers, and rolling down tricked-out pieces of modern two-wheeled art, lining them up, kicking them to life.

Food stands lift their covers and scrape their grills, heating the coals, getting ready for the day. "We go through about half a ton of hamburger meat during the week," I was told by one man with a relatively small roadside pitch.

Junction Avenue is intersected by narrow side streets and lined with houses, a blend of wood, brick, and stucco. Motorcycles are everywhere, parked in driveways, lined up on front lawns, chained to door handles and fences.

Willie Nelson's voice wafts out from an open window on Shepherd Street. The air smells of bacon and coffee.

Sturgis is waking up.

There's a tattoo studio on the corner of Sherman, its windows full of flash, featuring big tribal pieces in black, like zebra's stripes, biker murals with artist David Mann's famous Ghost Rider in pale blue and red streaking across a desert landscape, and the standard array of hearts, daggers, and naked ladies.

Look left, down Main and already there are hundreds of bikes parked in a long line, stretching from the watch

tower, past the Armory, all the way to the intersection at
Third. Some of the saloons are open and the sidewalks are
beginning to fill with people.

I feel like a stranger here, the same way I have felt in
so many of the other towns I've passed through. An observer, more connected to the road behind me than to this
epicenter of motorcycles and the people who ride them.

Ride on, across the light to Lazalle, turning left to ride
along a back drop of the forty- and fifty-foot trailers that
serve as traveling showrooms for bike and accessory companies from all over the United States. It costs $7–10
thousand to rent a space for the week and the object of
being here is not so much to sell product as to establish
a serious presence in the motorcycle world.

Sturgis, aside from being a big party, is also big business.

I ride to the light on Third and turn right, heading down
a block toward the Civic Center, where Senator Ben
Nighthorse Campbell gave his speech about the Black
Hills, to the end of the road, then a left into the parking
lot, where I am stopped by a steel chain and a uniformed
guard.

"Sorry sir, you will have to park your motorcycle and
come in by foot."

"But—"

The last thing I intend to do is leave the bike. It seems
absolutely necessary that after such a long ride I make it
all the way to Big Dog.

"—this bike is part of the Big Dog display."

He looks the bike over. It's covered in mud and dust,
in complete contrast to the acre of polished steel and
chrome that reflects the Morning sun, spreading out
against the macadam in front of me.

"Have you got a vendor's pass?"

"No."

"Wait here."

I sit behind the chain, waiting.

A few minutes later the guard reappears. Mohawk is walking beside him. His head has been restyled, the privet hedge chopped and polished, leaving a smiling billiard ball on top of his shoulders.

"Richard, we were wondering when you'd show up," he says, extending a hand.

Mohawk's handshake is my first real connection to Sturgis. It pulls me in from the highway and gives me a fast and certain sense of family.

"What happened to your head?" I ask.

"Too much maintenance," he answers. "Gave it the chop."

"How 'bout the Moshing?"

"Nearly broke my shoulder last May. I'm retired from the pit."

The chain is dropped and I follow Mohawk into the maze of trailers, across red carpets, past a hundred different configurations of frames, tanks, and engines. Riding slowly to avoid ploughing into any of the tattoos, engineer boots, ballooning biceps, or silicone breasts that have begun to filter across from Main Street.

The Big Dog trailer is red, with a matching marquee and carpet which runs its fifty-foot length. It occupies the entire corner of the lot, on the Lazalle side of the Civic Center's parking area. I see Sheldon first, wearing a leather Big Dog jacket, jeans, and running shoes. He's standing in front of a sleek red motorcycle, which is stretched, raked, very low to the ground, has billet aluminum wheels and what looks to me like an air spoiler molded to the bottom front section of its frame. He's talking to a customer and I hear him refer to the new bike as a Wolf and mention the price, $28,500. The guy doesn't balk, but he doesn't go for his wallet, either.

Sheldon looks up, sees me and smiles.

"You made it."

Nick Messer and Tim, Big Dog's sales director, hustle down the steps from the trailer. Both are big men, dressed in fresh denim, engineer boots, and Big Dog Sic'm T-shirts.

Messer takes a quick glance at the motorcycle as I shut it down and climb off.

"Bet you wished you had that windshield."

He walks to the bike, hovers a moment above the see-through dash, and presses a couple of buttons.

"2,477 miles."

I look down and see the figure on the digital display.

"I believe that's the longest trip anyone's ever done on one of our bikes," Messer says.

Before I can take a bow he adds, "Without a windshield."

We celebrate my arrival with a six pack of iced tea from the cooler, a couple of brotherly backslaps and a short jab to my midsection, delivered by Messer in a demonstration of the fighting skills he picked up during his military service in Okinawa. That and an armory of knives keep him safe from undesirable customers which is just as well since a particularly loud and hairy one has just arrived at my Silver Bike, which is sitting on the red carpet at Mohawk's end of the trailer, right beside the entrance ramp to the traveling service department.

UNCLE MILTY

THE SILVER BIKE LOOKS SMALL AND TIGHT, understated when compared to the flamed tanks and stretched frames that surround it.

"Milton's back," Messer says.

"Milton?"

He points to the grizzly gentleman slobbering over my saddle.

"He wants to buy your bike."

My bike? Milton wants to buy my bike. I haven't even laid hands on it, and Milton's after it. He's touching it, stroking the saddle. He's about to sit on it. *Milton?* The only other Milton I've ever heard of is the comedian Milton Berle, the late Uncle Milty, reported—by Marilyn Monroe—to have possessed the largest penis in Hollywood. *Milton? Climbing onto my sled.*

"Hold on a second," I say, making my way towards Milton's bodysuit of inked spider webs, eagles, and Ride to Live inscriptions.

Messer, fully armed and laughing, is right behind me.

Milton extends a hand, darkened by ink, and made
heavy by a kilo weight of silver rings.

"You the feller owns this thing?"

I latch on to a large skull and squeeze.

"Yes."

"How much?"

I glance down at the bike. The paint is fine and lacquered, giving a smooth uniformity between the Battistini
aluminum tank and the Milwaukee Iron steel fenders.
Every detail seems to flow together.

"It's not for sale."

Milton grins. His teeth are amazingly large and appear
to change color in the bright sunlight. A harlequin finish?
They look expensive.

"Not for *say-el*? Hell, everythin's for sale."

I reach down and touch the throttle grip.

"Not this."

"Name a price."

I meet his eyes, or more accurately, attempt to locate
them behind a bush of gray streaked beard and the dark,
round lenses of his glasses. He looks like ZZ Top on acid.

Milton continues to smile and I get the feeling that he's
baiting me.

"How much?"

I decide to call his bluff.

"Thirty-five thousand."

He reaches to his back pocket and pulls out a well worn
leather wallet. While this is happening two women emerge
from the corridors of chrome which lead from Lazelle.
Both are clad in black leather riding chaps and matching
thongs, causing a conspicuous amount of white and dim-
pled flesh to explode from the rear ends of their costumes.
They make way for Milton.

I know I'm in trouble when the first wedge of five-hundred-dollar bills appears. Just in time for the arrival of his cheering section.

"Give ya three grand on deposit."

He begins to peel the top layer from his wad.

"You bought if for me?" The blondest and largest of the platinum duo asks.

I cast a discreet glance at her riding chaps, picturing her ass spreading like cottage cheese against my hand-stitched saddle.

I fumble. "I was just—"

Messer steps in.

"Milton, we'll build you two more just like it."

Milton firms up. This is horse trading and obviously where he comes from, a deal's a deal.

The second blonde enters the fray.

"Then I get one, too," she says.

Milton looks hard at her.

"You promised," she adds, draping an arm around his shoulder and bouncing a hefty hip off his thigh.

"How long will it take?" Milton asks.

"Sixty days," Messer answers. "We can build you anything you want in sixty days."

"For both of 'em?"

"Yes, we can build both bikes in sixty days."

Milton looks down at the Silver Bike, as if he's making the painful decision whether or not to relinquish his stake in it.

"But *hay-el*, I like this here one."

So do I.

The Silver Bike is tailored to me, the culmination of everything I've been trying to do since buying the 883 Sportster at Warrs in London, fifteen years ago, back in the days when I was certain that four stick-on golden eagles and a sissy bar constituted a custom machine.

"Milton, it's not for sale," I say.

He's not listening.

"Beautiful bike," he says. "So plain, so simple."

Yes, and it's cost me about two hundred thousand dollars in motorcycles, a divorce, a change of country, a new life and the floods of Iowa to get to it. Simple, like that first silver bike, sitting beside the road in New Jersey, just a motorcycle.

"You think about it," Milton says, flashing me with his neon teeth. "I'll be back."

With a leathered lady under each jungle armpit he departs, as I turn to Messer for reassurance.

"He was a dental surgeon in Houston," Messer says. "Made a bundle and retired."

"Bullshit."

"It's the truth."

It is possible. I've met a well known cardiologist from Tulsa, Oklahoma, who looked every inch a hard-core biker. I've met a U.S. Senator in cutoffs, an Olympic gold medal athlete on a Harley, a pro wrestler on a Titan, a top fashion journalist having her tongue pierced, a movie icon on a Dresser, even an eighty-year-old ex–U.S. customs officer, covered head to toe in tattoos who informed me that he didn't get his first Harley till he was sixty-eight and his first tattoo till he was seventy. There was also the English lord, with a pierced scrotum and a cowbell dangling from it, standing on a barstool in Deadwood, ringing for another drink, prior to removal and a $90.00 fine by the local constabulary. There's nothing like a pair of beat-up engineer boots, dusty jeans, a T-shirt and, a motorcycle to obliterate any social or economic pretense. Milton could have been a dental surgeon. The question is, will he be back for my teeth?

Before I can voice my concerns, Messer suggests a

quick trip into town for a bite to eat and a stop at Lethal Steel, home of the tempered fighting knife. I wonder if he's trying to prepare me for attack.

Several burritos later and we're wading down Main Street, moving with the crush of people, past millions of dollars in rolling art, each customized or personalized and all loved. I'm stuck on a beautifully done copy of Captain America's Harley from the film *Easy Rider,* wondering whether it's one of the California Motorcycle Co. replicas that they intend to build as a limited edition, when I bump smack into a couple of old friends, encased in double-D cups.

"Richard."

"Lori."

Ron, her husband, snaps a few photos as we embrace. I ask how the *Easyriders* rodeo circuit has been treating her and she answers that she and Ron have been having a ball, traveling from state to state, bike show to bike show, with the *Easyriders* crew. As Fox of the Year, Lori has been in constant demand. As the man financially responsible for her assets, Ron is justifiably proud. Both are relaxed, good time people and I admire Ron's ability to detach himself from the hordes of two-wheeled cowboys determined to affix Lori to the back of their saddles. Lori flaunts it and flirts with it, but she's always a lady. "Best investment I ever made," Ron says, eyeing Lori's bosom, as another enthusiast elbows in for a picture.

Which makes me reconsider: Ron was a successful veterinarian before his midlife lifestyle change. Maybe Milton was a dental surgeon.

Messer and I move on, leaving Ron with his camera and Lori surrounded by fans.

Down Main, into a small side street, then a quick duck into a single-roomed shop where we are greeted by a tall, sinewy man carrying his right arm in a sling and his hand in heavy bandages.

"Luke, what happened?" Messer asks.

"Practicing yesterday with a live blade, missed my timing and got caught with a horizontal slash. Cut my hand and my elbow clean to the bone, lucky he missed the artery."

Messer introduces us, foregoing the handshake, after which we examine an assortment of knives ranging from a fourteen-inch Bowie to a particularly vicious little number that resembles a corkscrew with a three-inch blade, its small knurled handle made to fit lengthwise across the palm of the hand so it can be used with a continuous punching action.

"Damascus-style steel, pounded and folded like a Samurai sword," our injured host informs me, holding the Bowie up to the light so I'm able to fully appreciate the delicate rolls in the surface of the metal.

There are also a wide assortment of surgical steel knives, "sharp as scalpels," that double as belt buckles until that magic moment of revelation.

I'm tempted to whip out my Timberline, which I believe is equal to anything at Lethal Steel in the design category but, with only a three-and-a-half-inch blade, I suffer a bout of locker room anxiety and keep it in my boot.

Messer keeps returning to the big Bowie with the ebony handle and the Damascus-style blade. It is beautiful, and he does collect them, but the price of $450 seems to be a stumbling block. He holds it, balanced in his palm, grips the handle and gently stirs the air with a few slow motion slashes before returning it to its leather sheath.

"I'll think about it," he says.

"Just not sure about the weight distribution," he comments to me as we depart, leaving Luke to change his bandages. "Seemed to be a little heavy in the hilt."

We arrive back at Big Dog headquarters in time to see Sheldon, flanked by Tim, bending down beside the engine of the Wolf, attempting to make a point to Milton, who is now hovering above the new red bike. I hear the boss say something about the Wolf's hidden suspension, giving it the look of a rigid frame, and Milton nods approvingly. His thonged companions are nowhere in sight and, as before, he looks like a man who has come to do business. I breathe a sigh of relief as his heavily adorned fingers caress the Wolf's silhouette saddle, thinking that there could be a shift in his affections. That is, until he sees me.

Then the neon smile explodes, the wallet is drawn like a six gun and the engineer boots slam like sledgehammers against the welcome mat as he strides in my direction.

"I want it."

Fortified by my visit to Lethal Steel, and newly appreciative of my small but perfectly formed Timberline, I answer.

"It's not for sale."

"Bullshit."

"At any price."

Milton is, for once, speechless and I watch his lower lip pout from deep within the recesses of his beard. His wallet, half cocked, falls to his side.

I use the opportunity to press my advantage.

"Were you really a dental surgeon?"

I believe he meets my eyes, although it's tough to tell what's going on below the dark surfaces of his glasses.

"Hell no."

"Then what—"

"I'm a rabbi," he says, poker-faced.

"Give me a break."

His lips part and his teeth loom in a Vegas billboard of a smile.

"Nightclubs. I own a few nightclubs."

That makes sense, at least more sense than dental surgery, although it doesn't explain his teeth. Before I launch into further inquiry another voice, every bit as voluminous as Milton's, catches me from behind.

"Hey amigo."

Oh no. Milton and Big Jim, under the same marquee.

I turn to see my new business partner step onto the carpet, with Nancy and Gary a pace behind. His ostrich skins appear slightly more worn than they did when I last laid eyes on them in Dallas and his hair is braided into a stately silver gray rope that touches the seat of his jeans. Nancy looks annoyed—as she usually is with Jim—and Gary's shoulders seem broader.

"Bet you're glad you had that rainsuit," he says before engulfing me in a Texas-sized bear hug.

There's been rain here, too. Maybe that's Nancy's problem.

Embraces all around and Milton is temporarily forced to the sidelines. Finally I introduce him but his primary interest remains with the acquisition of the Silver Bike. An obvious obsession has set in. The condition, formerly termed Hog Fever, would probably in this case best be described as Rabid Dog Syndrome.

"Give ya thirty-six right now," he says.

The figure stuns me to silence, but Big Jim, sniffing money, answers the challenge.

"You ever read Richard's book?"

"Book? What book? You write books?"

Jim produces a copy of the midlife gospel from somewhere inside his riding jacket and hands it over.

Milton studies the cover.

"That you?"

"Yes," I say.

"Mind if I keep it?"

Since I'll never sell him the bike, I feel I owe him something.

"It's yours."

"Signed by the author," Jim adds.

"Thanks," Milton answers. Then, before Jim can close the sale, "I'll be back for the bike."

He turns abruptly and walks away, in the direction of Lazalle, studying the cover of the book and occasionally turning to look at me, as if he doesn't quite trust his own eyes.

"Owns a string of nightclubs," I explain, watching him depart.

"Whorehouses more likely," Jim grumbles.

Nancy shakes her head. "Why are you always so negative?"

"He didn't pay for that book."

"I don't think anybody's paid for one yet," Nancy answers.

"Well, that's all gonna change tonight," Jim assures, wrapping me under the new tattoo on his right shoulder. "We got a signing at the campground."

I can hardly wait.

THE SIGNING

MOWHAWK NEEDS A LITTLE TIME WITH THE SILVER BIKE —
checking fluids, adjusting the jets on the carb, etc.—
before I take off on it, so I stick with the Harlequin
Cruiser for my first night at the campground.

Gary's six-cylinder Valkyrie leads us down Lazalle, west
to Route 90 and on towards Spearfish. There are bikes
everywhere, going in every direction. It's rare to see a car.

Nancy rides beside him on her black Softail and Big
Jim, mounted on my old Springer, is directly in front of
me.

I study him in the way a jealous husband might view
his adulterous wife and lover through a keyhole in the
bedroom door.

There is something obscene in the way his threadbare
denims settle into my old saddle and the manner in which
his long legs bow out at the knee as those ostrich skins
point skyward against the foot pegs. He looks too big for
the bike. For *my* bike. Showing off, bucking and prancing,
every now and then glancing back at me.

"Damn clutch. I'll never get used to it!" he shouts.

Bastard. Riding my bike like he owns it . . . He does own it.

Big Jim. Another Highway Buddha, teaching me another lesson, this one in the pain of possessiveness. *Let it go,* I tell myself. *It's over. That part of your life is over, that gargantuan temperamental bored-out expense is gone, along with the ex-wife, the big house, the show biz parties.* But it's not, not completely. It's right in front of me, spitting fumes in my face, with the silver-haired evangelist in the saddle.

"Damn, this thing's got some grunt!"

And damn, I still want it stuffed and mounted like a trophy in my living room.

The campground looks like a Gypsy outpost. Every level of recreational vehicle is there, from the rusted out camper with a laundry line baring jockey shorts and white socks stretching from its screened door to a nearby tree to a wood paneled monster, as long as the Big Dog trailer, that looks like a luxury yacht, with twin satellite dishes mounted like radar reflectors on its roof.

"Belongs to a Chinese industrialist," Jim says, as we slow for another speed bump. "All teak inside, three bedrooms, an exercise pool, and a media room."

I stare at the million-dollar behemoth, wondering how Jim has managed to infiltrate its infrastructure and also wondering whether the owner has a copy of my book, and if he's paid for it.

"Don't even think the guy owns a bike," Jim says.

"Probably a drug lord," Gary comments.

I picture Milton inside the wooden enclave, counting piles of bills and plotting to take over my Silver Bike.

Jim backs off on the throttle as we follow him through acres of campsites, past picnic tables, barbecues and

American flags, bumping along to the beat of a hundred boom boxes, belting out everything from John Mellencamp's "Little Pink Houses" to Dwight Yoakam's "Fast as You." With the exception of the bike-less Chinese industrialist (whose navigational system may have malfunctioned causing him to end up here, surrounded) and Gary's Valkyrie, we are in the heartland of patriotic America, a microcosm of the dream. Country music, v-twin engines, hot dogs, and Budweiser, all flowing into one free, full-throated revving harmony.

Jim begins to wave and exchange greetings with people as we ride into the section of this temporary community that constitutes his home, for bike week.

To my right, about a hundred yards away I can make out something that looks remarkably like the Colonel's *Hog Fever* banner, last seen unfurled above our heads at Sturgis in the Village.

"Tom sent it to me, thought it might come in handy for promotions," Jim says.

I recall the corporate offices, the Colonel's Stetson, his Camel Lights, and the stacks of books that insulated his garage through that long cold winter. Now, he's back to a straight job, has quit smoking, and in a last gesture of good will—or sanity—has passed the *Hog Fever* banner on to Big Jim.

The banner is mounted on twin poles on the roof of the silver camper. There is also a small marquee above the entrance steps, a cardboard sign announcing the book signing, and a bath mat–sized red carpet below the last step. Somehow giving the impression of a roadside shrine.

We park and dismount. Nancy heads at once for the ice cooler which stands to the side of the camper and Gary takes his post as grill man, lighting the coals for the night's festivities. Jim beckons me inside the camper.

It is a shrine.

Autographed pictures of biker friends and dirt track racers line the walls, along with a dozen candles. There's a Dallas HOG chapter flag hanging on the wall near the door and an American flag at the far end, along with a stack of boxes.

"Brought two thousand copies of the book," Jim says.

And a king-sized mattress which takes up most of the floor, with several pillows and a Navajo rug draped over it. I ponder Jim's use of space.

"Nancy likes a big bed," he says.

Outside, our flight attendant has brewed up a gallon jug of margaritas and Gary is unwrapping several pounds of spare ribs from their cellophane protection. I take the opportunity to return the rainsuit and apologize for the slight tear in the seat, which Jim assures me is no problem.

"Her ass is gettin' bigger every day anyway," he says.

Nancy smacks him.

Our first guest arrives while we are laying out the paper plates on the large, folding table. She is dressed in jeans, a bra, and carries a bar of soap and a towel. She is very wobbly on her bare feet.

Jim heads her off at the jug.

"Annie, you come to buy a book?"

Annie looks confused.

"Came to take a shower but I wouldn't mind another drink."

"Shower room's that way, through the trees at the back. You'll see an opening in the bush, then a sign for the public toilets."

Annie weaves on by and disappears behind the camper.

"Girl's been drunk for three days," Jim says.

The sound of engines turning over has begun to dominate the homogeneous mix of rock, country and blues that settles with the humidity in the air. People, dressed in denim and leather, are riding by, heading out of the camp-site.

"Do you really think anybody's going to show up?" I ask.

With pro wrestling, famous bands, and a hundred sa-loons filled with gyrating bodies, I think we've got major competition in the events department. Even John Kaye and Steppenwolf have dusted off the cobwebs for a ren-dition of "Born to Be Wild," at the Buffalo Chip Camp-ground. Last time I heard them was in 1985, when my old band was opening for Steppenwolf at the Brandywine Club in Philadelphia. There were three hundred Harleys in the parking lot, and as many outlaws sitting out front waiting impatiently for Kaye to get up and wail their an-them. I was on stage for forty-five torturous minutes, draped in an American flag, singing originals—that no-body had ever heard. Hoping like hell I wouldn't be as-sassinated. Now he's back, doing me in again.

"I've got commitments," Big Jim says.

Not long afterward a few of Jim's commitments straggle in. Nancy serves up in paper cups, Jim hits the button on the CD player, Willie Nelson sings and the party's under-way.

There's Sam and his wife from Milwaukee, Jeb and Iris from Myrtle Beach, Art from the camper directly across the road, who is looking for Annie and his towel, and Ted from Baton Rouge. Three books exchange hands quickly, one on consignment, and one on sale or return, depending on whether Jeb's brother Rick likes it, since Jeb doesn't read anything but *Popular Mechanics*. One is paid for in cash, which Big Jim pockets quickly, accompanied by a flick of his tongue.

Another arrival, by Honda Goldwing, and the joint is jumpin'. Andy and Sue have ridden down from Seattle and although he didn't bring his wallet they take two books on credit.

"We're raking it in," Jim says.

Gary is sweating, slinging ribs and Ted, who has not committed to a book, has seated himself in a folding chair by the welcome mat in front of the camper. He has, however, committed himself to a one-man assault on the margarita jug. He motions me over.

His voice is low and modulated.

"Sit down, sit down. We've got to talk."

I join him on the ground.

"You're a writer, heh?"

There's something conspiratorial in his tone, like he may have inside info on a crashed U.F.O.

I answer with a guarded "yes."

"You rich?"

"Not exactly."

"Thought writers made a lot of money."

"Some do, some don't. Having a best-seller is a little bit like winning the lottery."

"Do you want to make some big money?"

THE RAC

"SURE I'D LIKE TO MAKE SOME BIG MONEY." He reaches a short, thick hand into the top pocket of his overalls and produces a crumpled business card, which he hands to me.

THEODORE DOUGLAS SNARK, INVENTOR. That, along with a phone and fax number are embossed in gold on the ivory paper.

His sharp, narrow eyes await my reaction.

"An inventor?"

He nods his head.

"See that motorcycle over there?" he asks, pointing to the Springer.

"Yes."

"See that thing on the side of the engine?"

"You mean the carburetor?"

"Yeah."

"It's an S&S Super E," I say.

"Right, and if you took off the cover what would you find?"

"An air cleaner."

He pauses and takes a long swig from his paper cup.

"That is correct," he says.

I meet his eyes. His head is nodding. Should I sense a certain awe? Am I in the presence of greatness?

"Did you invent the air cleaner?"

"I invented the RAC," he answers.

I sift through my brain for technical support but come up short.

"I don't know what that is," I confess.

He bends closer, until I can smell the tequila on his breath. If I lit a match, he'd explode.

He whispers. "Rectal air cleaner."

"What?"

"A fart filter. Charcoal fiber, bound in gauze with an adhesive backing. Fits right over the crack in your ass like a sanitary napkin."

I'm not sure whether to laugh or not.

"I'm looking for investors."

If he's putting me on he's very good, because I don't detect even the hint of deception.

"You could fart with complete impunity."

"How about the noise?" I ask.

"I'm working on a baffle. The problem is size and weight but I'll get there."

He is serious. I can tell by his eyes and the dead set of his jaw.

"As an investor, you could get in at the bottom."

My reply is put on hold by Big Jim's arrival, offering me a paper plate containing a few pounds of spare ribs and a small mountain of coleslaw.

"Sixty-six," Jim says.

"Books?"

"Bucks. We've sold three of 'em."

"I hope you're not disappointed," I say.

"Hell no. I'm just gettin' started."

Jim eyes Ted.

"You bought one yet?"

Ted withdraws into the slung canvas seat of his chair.

"Pick one up before you leave," Jim says.

Ted assures him that he will, and there is an awkward gap in conversation which I fill by excusing myself. By the time I reach the jug, Ted is out for the count, and Annie has reappeared.

Judging by her bra, soap, and dry towel, she never found the shower.

"Great party on the other side of the hedge," she blurts before collapsing against the picnic table. Art is disgusted. He snaps up the soap and the towel and leaves her sprawled while he makes way for the hole in the hedge.

"I need a bath," he says.

By now it's ten o'clock and, with few exceptions, the campsite is in a high state of arousal. There's music, dancing, laughter, a series of grunts and snores from the Ted the inventor, who is no doubt fitted with a prototype RAC, and a brisk trade in loaner books.

Unfortunately, I am one of the few exceptions to the party. Having exceeded my new bedtime by three hours, I'm slurring my speech, limping on my injured knee, and yawning uncontrollably.

Gary, a true brother despite his Valkyrie, steps away from the grill, unfolds Annie from the bench and lays her out on the ground before walking to me. He drapes a heavy arm around my shoulder.

"Bro Richard, if you're tired go ahead over and sleep in my camper. There's a spare bed just off the kitchen. The door's open."

SHOTGUN WILLY'S

MY NEW ACCOMMODATIONS ARE TIGHT BUT THE BED is rock solid—not unusual for a metal slab—and there's a light breeze blowing through the screen door. The highway lullaby of a thousand bikes has been replaced by multiple CDs playing different songs. I try to tune in on one. It's Bob Dylan, singing "Tangled up In Blue."

"We'll meet again someday on the avenue . . ."

I hang on to his nasal lyric by a thread, until the thread breaks and I drift into the darkness.

Awakened by what feels like the rumbling gait of a large critter, maybe a bison or a bear, roaming around inside the camper, causing the floor to shift with each thunderous footstep.

I sit up, smacking my head against the windowsill.

My eyes adjust to the darkness. It's Gary, clad in his socks, T-shirt, and undershorts, moving menacingly towards the door.

"What's happening?"

"*Day-am,*" he says. "Listen to that."

I readjust my ears to the night. The cacophony of music

has died, replaced by laughter, and what sounds like a tussle taking place nearby. A few thumps and thuds, more laughter, a man's voice, a woman's.

Gary's body fills the entire frame of the front door as he stares out.

"Is there a problem?" I ask.

"Not for Jim and Nancy," he says.

"What?"

Gary sounds pissed off and I wonder if the king-sized bed in Jim's tabernacle has offended his sensitivities. More likely the noise is keeping him awake.

"So what?"

"Day-am," Gary repeats.

He's pulling on his jeans, tugging his boots up, stomping the floor. I'm afraid he's about to launch an assault on Jim, Nancy, and the book warehouse.

"Gary, what are you doing?"

"Goin' out. Want to come?"

"Where?"

He looks at me and smiles.

"Shotgun Willy's."

THE SCOUT

I LISTEN AS HIS EXHAUST PIPES fade in the distance. There's silence from the book emporium, and as I look out the window above my bunk I see the night sky is a canopy of stars.

I turn on the small reading light above my head, reach for my jeans, dig out my wallet, and remove the Chuck E. Cheese portrait of my son and pregnant wife.

Could I have ever guessed from that first ride that all this would happen?

There were a few more rides after Mrs. P's. A trip to the coast at Brighton in the pouring rain, several shorter excursions, many roadside stops for whiskey, and a lot of conversation. During that time she broke up with her boyfriend and I, still battling my ex-wife and having become a veteran of the damaged heart, became a sounding board, a father figure who felt anything but fatherly. Did she know how I really felt about her? I decided she had to. Life had become too short for pretense. I needed honesty. My urgency was compounded by the fact that my father was dying. It had happened quickly. Just before his eighty-second birthday he had been sharp and spry. He could still run up a flight of stairs. I had joked about his knee joints being better than my own traumatized hinges. The only thing that troubled him was a cough and sore throat that would not go away. Finally, he had a chest X ray.

I remember calling him from London to wish him a happy birthday.

"Hi, Champ."

His voice sounded a little more raspy than usual, but still full of his usual dry humor.

"Happy birthday, Scout."

"Guess what I got for a present?"

Something sounded wrong.

"What?"

"The big C," he said. "In my lungs."

It was like a kick in the gut.

"I'm sorry," was all I could say.

Six months of chemotherapy, bedside oxygen tanks and visits to the emergency room later and the Scout, minus much of the full head of hair he'd held on to for his entire life and thirty pounds of body weight lighter, was rigged up to the morphine drip to ease his pain.

"He has a week, maybe two," the ward nurse told me when I called.

That was on a Friday, so I booked a flight for the following Monday. I chose Monday because Sunday was going to be a special day. It had been planned for weeks. I was going to spend Sunday at my friend's flat. I was going to tell her, finally, how I felt about her. It was all or nothing. If she fell over from shock or laughed at me at least it would be out in the open and I could quit my charade of being the older buddy. The fact that my father was dying added to my sense that life was too short for games.

On Saturday morning my brother called.

"You ought to get over here," he said. "Dad isn't going to last much longer."

I called my father at the hospital. His voice was weak but still managed to lift when I told him that his manuscript, a detective novel he'd been working on since he'd retired from advertising, had received rave reviews from my editor in London.

"Do you think you'll be ready for the promotional tour?" I asked.

"Sure thing."

"We'll talk about it Monday," I promised.

"See you then, Champ," he said.

He didn't sound like a dying man.

When I spoke to the nurse, she reconfirmed that the scout wasn't going anywhere for the next couple of weeks. Still, my brother is insightful and he'd said, "get over here."

I struggled with my need to go and my need to stay. I felt compelled to get certain things straight. Sunday seemed to be critical in doing that. Sunday had become D-Day in my fight for change. I was afraid that if I missed Sunday, I would miss the rest of my life.

I did not change my flight.

I woke up on that day with my brother's voice still in my head, telling me to get home to Philadelphia, to get to dad. Yet, I had this other feeling, that I would never have this chance again, this chance to come clean.

I went to her apartment with the conflicting feelings battling inside me. I drank to cover them. Loosened up enough to tell her how I felt, about myself, about her, and about my father. It turned out she had lost her stepfather, the man who had raised her, to cancer. She seemed to know my heart. I spent the day with her, but in my mind I kept seeing the Scout lying in a bed, waiting for his oldest son to show up. *Hold on Scout, I'm coming.*

He died that day.

That has been my secret, the guilt I've carried ever since, all the way out here to Sturgis.

Gary's camper is a strange place to come to terms with something so deep and so private, but here I am, and here it is, as sure as the stars in the sky.

"Dad, I'm sorry I wasn't there for you. I'm sorry."

I lay still, lost in a deep sadness.

Until I hear his voice, as clearly as if he were standing beside me.

"Son, the day I died was the day you began to take control of your life. It was the day you became a man. Take another look at that picture in your hand."

I do.

"Take good care of my grandchildren."

A sense of peace fills me and a sense of forgiveness.

DAY SEVEN

MAN'S MAIN TASK IN LIFE IS TO GIVE
BIRTH TO HIMSELF.

—ERIC FROMM, PSYCHOANALYST

SIMPLY RIDING

THE BISON HAS RETURNED, HIS SNORES reverberating off the walls at the opposite end of the camper, his dusty jeans draped next to a box of Cheerios on the breakfast table and his snakeskin boots standing tall and empty beside his bed.

Outside, the world is hung over. Doors are opening on tentative hinges, voices are soft and repentant, and bike chains clank as locks are tumbled. There's the occasional rumble of an engine starting but even those sound distant and baffled.

I lift my head, careful of the windowsill, and peer out. The sky is clear and pale blue. It's already hot.

The voice of the evangelist calls from beyond the aluminum-sided walls.

"Anybody alive in there?"

I slip from beneath my thin blanket and land lightly on the floor, trying not disturb the late-night reveler in the master bunk.

"Still a few ribs left over from last night and I think there's even something left in the jug."

I stare at him through the screen.

His tone changes. "Nancy's got a pot of coffee going."

Into my clothes, a quick trip through the hedges, and the day officially begins.

By the time we've hosed off the bikes and given them a quick once-over with the polishing rag, Gary is dressed and complaining.

"*Day-um* if I'm gonna stand in a line waitin' for a place to sit down in some girlie bar. Girls was too tired to work anyway. They were wasted. I'm never going back. This place's got too many people in it."

"Yeah, and they're all as old as we are," Jim adds, surveying the haggard faces of his neighbors across the road. Art is outside, looking up at the sky, apparently checking weather conditions and Annie's got the soap and towel again. She looks determinedly past us, towards the hole in the hedge. "Be nice to see some young stuff for a change. Sorry, Nancy."

"That's alright, Jim, no young stuff would want your old bones anyway."

"At least it isn't raining," Gary comments.

"You'd be surprised," Jim says.

I'm not sure if he's talking about the weather or his ability to attract younger women, but I do notice he has rolled his full Dresser down from the back of his trailer. Leaving the Springer chained to the front step of the book emporium.

"Anything over twenty miles and I like to travel in comfort," he explains.

"That's because you're an old man," Nancy adds.

Several mugs of caffeine later and the team is saddled and riding across speed bumps, past the mysterious teak motor home with its roof-mounted, satellite-controlled tracking system and Dr. Fu Manchu hidden behind curtained windows, out and on to the main road.

Stopping in the town of Spearfish long enough for Gary to lay down a hundred bucks with the Chamber of Commerce in a raffle for a new Harley Road King.

"Do you really think you've got a chance?" Jim asks.

"I'm going to win it," Gary answers, sounding like a man who knows the fix is in.

By the time we arrive at Big Dog, it's already eleven o'clock and Sheldon and the crew, looking clean, shaved and freshly pressed, are in full swing, plus there's another face amongst them. This guy is everything Fabio has ever wanted to be, with a handsomely chiseled face, a great white smile, a lush blanket of dark hair and a torso fashioned on Mt. Olympus.

"Finally, one for the ladies," Nancy whispers just before we're introduced to Richard, who has just ridden in from Aspen on a flamed Big Dog.

He may be Godlike, he may be young, and he may have eighteen-inch arms. He may have a windshield and a good sense of humor. He may even have my first name, but damn it, he hasn't ridden 2,500 miles in Nancy's rainsuit. At least that's what I tell myself as I shake his hand.

Big Jim remains on the the periphery of the action, eyeing Richard's triceps and searching for character flaws.

I leave Nancy and several other ladies (who seem to be swarming in from Lazalle), examining Richard, who turns out to be one of Aspen's premier personal trainers, and sidestep my way to the service end of the trailer where the Silver Bike is primed and ready to roll. Mounted on the tail end of the red carpet, it looks like a jewel shining in the sun and in a rare moment of privacy, with Milton nowhere in sight and Richard serving as a diversion, I admire it from several different angles.

I continue my admiration while Mohawk, unmoved by the throng of ladies circling Richard's deltoids, removes the plates from the Harlequin Cruiser and bolts them on, then bends and lets some air out of the back tire.

"That should give you a little bit of rear suspension," he explains.

Messer finishes with a customer, circumnavigates the female crowd, and walks briskly towards me. I brace myself for either a horizontal slash with his new Bowie or a straight right to the solar plexus. He's smiling, always a dangerous sign. I take a step backwards, using Gary as a shield.

"Sold three Pit Bulls this morning," he says.

The Pit Bull is Big Dog's rigid frame bike. In many ways, with its reversed front forks, drag bars, fat back tire and 107 cubic inch engine, it resembles the Silver Bike.

"That's great," I answer.

"All to Milton."

"You're kidding?"

"Paid the deposit in cash. Ten thousand bucks."

"He definitely runs a string of whorehouses," Jim says.

Gary perks up. "Maybe he can get me a table at Shotgun's."

I look at the Silver Bike.

"I'm safe?"

"For the time being," Messer answers. "Though he's still threatening to come back for yours."

"I'd better get out of town."

Jim and Nancy are going to the races later in the afternoon. Scotty Parker, nine-time national champion, is riding the half mile dirt track and Jim's a devoted fan. Gary has plans to stake a claim at one of the two bars inside the Easyriders Full Throttle Saloon, and I've been offered floor space for the night at the Big Dog ranch house—

next to the other Richard—which is a six-thousand-dollar-a-week three-bedroom rental with the owner stationed in a house trailer in the adjacent lot, just to keep an eye on things.

"Let's head for Deadwood," Jim suggests. "Hey Nancy. We're leaving!"

If I was riding high in the saddle on the Cruiser, I'm back on the street with the Silver Bike, connected by my kidneys to every bump and twist in the uneven surface of Lazalle. Have I done it again? Is this going to be another bike that I love to look at but hate to ride? Like the Battistini stretch, which was great in photographs, but nearly impossible to navigate around a corner. At least this frame is short enough for me to reach the front pegs without extensions on my cowboy boots, and it does seem to handle in its own muscular way, not exactly flexible but with its low center of gravity and overload of torque it is certainly responsive. And the sound? Sweet, low and mean through the straight pipes.

"Thing's got some grunt," Jim comments as I pull even with him.

It sure does and with the engine already broken in it feels like it wants to go.

Out on Route 90 the road surface evens. I look around. Not a cop in sight. I accelerate. A hundred is nothing. It's there before I even look down at the micro gauges. A hundred and ten, twenty, no problem. I reckon the Silver Bike is a hundred pounds lighter than the cruiser, about as basic as two wheels and an engine can get, and the gear ratio is set for the fast burst, the quarter mile.

I slow down then hit it one more time. The back tire squeals, spits a little dirt and my ass is nearly on the rear fender.

"Gonna get yourself arrested!" Jim shouts.

He's right, but this is fun, and as long as the road is smooth I don't even notice the lack of rear springs. I'm complimenting my own good taste, designmanship, lower lumbar fortitude and Mohawk's rear tire pressure technique when I hit a pockmark-sized pothole that sends me flying. Bumping down, winded, I realize that the Silver Bike is going to require a shade more road surface awareness than I've been used to for the past 2,500 miles. In other words, I'd better watch where I'm going. Riding a rigid is sort of like walking barefoot, enjoyable as long as you know your terrain. There's no better way to feel connected to the road than to be virtually sitting on it and the stories of bikers in the fifties and sixties riding rigid-framed motorcycles from coast to coast can only be appreciated by spending a couple of hours on top of one. It's probably the only time in motorsport that a fat ass is a distinct advantage.

We pull off Route 90, opting for the scenic two lane highway through Boulder Canyon, riding through gorges, past waterfalls, and up and down the sides of mountains. Everything is lush and green and the air is so clean and fresh that it feels like it's washing the sins of fat foods, alcohol and secondhand smoke from my skin.

The Silver Bike pulls like a tractor, carrying me around the corners without much alteration in the steering. It's got its own way of taking the road, following the natural bank of the highway, hugging it with its gigantic rear tire while the Ceriani front forks, originally designed for racing, adjust to the slightest changes in grade and minimize the feeling that the bike is shimmying or sliding as it winds round the bends. The sound from the pipes, reverberating off the rock walls that have been cut through the pass, is like a .50-caliber machine gun, with a throaty backfire when I back off on the throttle. It's biker music.

We are not alone in the canyon, in fact there are hundreds of other motorcycles, traveling in either direction, but the processions are orderly and the speed is controlled. Fifty is too fast along these roads but 30 or 40 m.p.h. allows both the sensation of speed and the appreciation of the environment. The hills and dips are demanding enough to require full attention but slow enough that nothing is missed in the blur.

We come out of the canyon on the east side of Deadwood, looking down at a long strip of wood-framed hotels, restaurants and glass-fronted saloons. This was the last stop for James Butler "Wild Bill" Hickock, who was killed here in 1876, and the town, named for the dead trees that were found in the narrow canyon of Deadwood Gulch, revolves around the lumber industry, and mining for gold. It's a gambling haven and Kevin Costner, following his film *Dances With Wolves,* purchased a prominent saloon—which he still owns—on Main Street. Usually the population of Deadwood is just under 2,000, but today, beneath a blare of sun that has already pushed the thermometer above the hundred mark, there are at least that many people walking the streets, and as many steel horses parked in the lot in the center of town. Even as we ride through, slowing so that the heat envelops us, I have the sensation that we've ridden into a time warp and come out in the last quarter of the nineteenth century. There is soul here, unspoiled by tourism. Cowboy soul.

"It's too hot to stop," Jim says.

"Too many people," Gary adds.

Which is the wonderful thing about this week of the year. With all the people and congestion in Sturgis and all of the surrounding towns, there is the solitude of the Black Hills, and the ride, always the ride.

We continue through town and pick up Highway 385 south. The road is another two-laner that cuts through the Hills, which are so green they look almost blue beneath the sun.

I have the sense that we have been assimilated by the atmosphere of the place—taken in and embraced—our visit recorded forever by granite eyes as old as the hills themselves. I feel small and insignificant, yet at the same time empowered by the vastness of the expanses and the unspoiled beauty of the great jagged rock faces and ancient trees.

Passing through Hill City, where we pick up Highway 16, traveling with the silvery blue waters of Lake Patola and Lake Sheridan to either side, beneath the eyes of Crazy Horse, the old Lakota Sioux warrior. His sculpture was begun in 1938 by Korczak Ziolkowski. Today, continued by his children and grandchildren, it consumes an entire mountain and sits 563 feet above the valley of Laughing Water. It is the largest monument on the face of the earth.

The bikes roll on.

Into Custer, the oldest settlement in the Black Hills. The town, named for General George Armstrong Custer, is small but the main street running through it seems disproportionately wide. In fact it is one hundred and fifty feet from curb to curb and was built this way, or so Jim informs me, so that eight yoke of oxen (two oxen bound together by a yoke) could make a U-turn in the middle of the street.

Today, the only things making U-turns on Main Street are motorcycles, hundreds of them.

We park in front of a cafe-bar that has tables on the sidewalk, then settle back with four bottles of Corona, paid for with the profits of last night's signing. There seem to be more riders here and less spectacle in the flesh department than in Sturgis, as if the grandeur of the surrounding Black Hills has instilled a quiet respect and humility to those who ride through them.

The day is hot and lazy and the eighty miles of riding has massaged our minds into a place that doesn't require much speech, so we sit and watch the sidewalk parade and the various incarnations of bikes as they come and go.

It's three o'clock by the time Jim checks his watch.

"If we're going to see Scotty ride, we'd better hit the road," he says.

Gary and Nancy agree, but I don't feel like moving.

I've got that feeling again. No deadline, no place I've got to be. The Silver Bike looks right at home, parked with the pack, in front of the cafe.

We agree to meet tomorrow at the Big Dog trailer, then I watch my friends climb into the saddles of their bikes, start up and U-turn back toward the highway.

It feels natural to be on my own again. I've got hours of good light left and all the great road I could ever want. I have another Corona. Finally, it's just me and the Silver Bike, like two old friends who haven't seen each other in a long time, anxious to spend some time together, alone.

By the time I leave Custer, headed north on 385, the sun has begun its slow Western arc and the air has cooled.

I'm riding.

Whipping along at sixty-five, bouncing up and down against the saddle and feeling every joint in the surface of the road. Conscious of everything from the wind in my face to the smells of leaves and grass, dried from a summer drought and blowing past me. Knowing myself better than I did twenty-five hundred miles ago, understanding myself as a son, a husband, a father, and a man. At peace. Enjoying this moment of solitude. Me and the Silver Bike, joined at the hip, with time dissolving all around us. Feeling once again, as I did thirty-five years ago on my first ride, as if I've found the center of the universe.

Riding, simply riding.

EPILOGUE

YOU CAN'T ALWAYS GET WHAT YOU WANT,
BUT IF YOU TRY SOMETIMES YOU JUST
MIGHT FIND, YOU'LL GET WHAT YOU NEED.

—THE ROLLING STONES

SEDONA

FOLLOWING STURGIS, I HEADED SOUTHWEST to Sedona, Arizona, and booked into the Cloud House, which is a meditation retreat set at the base of the red mountains surrounding the town. It was a drastic shift, from the energy of a half-million bikers to the solitude of one. There was a rope chair on the porch of my room, like a swing, suspended from the ceiling. I spent a lot of time in that chair, looking at the mountains and letting my mind drift, while the contents of my saddlebags were laid out on the wooden bench at the foot of my bed: shirts and jeans, flashlight, a knife, a cell phone, socks, shampoo, sunglasses, goggles, a set of ratchets, a diary, the espadrilles, the leather jacket, all kinds of stuff, some relevant, some just extra weight. As the week went by, those contents became significant. They represented what I thought I had needed at the beginning of my journey and what, in fact, I actually did need. In the clarity of the setting, that became a metaphor for my life.

I returned to Long Island in late August.

The ride had never been intended as a life-changing

experience. Compared to many rides that many have taken, it was a short journey. I had set out to escape the daily routine, to have a little adventure, maybe even recapture a bit of my youth. I was on the road to the Silver Bike.

What actually happened was quite different. The miles and the hours alone provided a space to have a dialogue with myself, to become acquainted with the man I had become. It provided opportunity to confront some of the things I had been avoiding and to take a look at others from a fresh perspective.

Back home, I was more at ease and more forgiving. Inside, I had less anger, fewer questions, and a greater understanding of the things I had done during my life, the decisions I had made, and the roads I had taken. I also felt a greater responsibility to be honest with myself.

I realized how important my family was to me, how they tested, nurtured, and defined me.

Our reunion was terrific.

Again, the detours made sense.

They had led me in a complete circle, to a place that was home.

On March 21st, 2000, Tomas Richard La Plante was born.

The Colonel still has a few "No Cure" T-shirts available.

Big Jim has been relegated to cyberspace. Contact him at www.hogfever.com.

Nancy is flying.

Big Dog has upped production, probably because of Milton.

Gary won the Road King.

The Silver Bike is in the garage, with a full tank, ready to ride.